THE QUEST FOR THE
HOLY GRILL

The Quest for the
Holy Grill

50 Crummy But Good Restaurants within Rambling Range of Washington, D.C.

Donovan Kelly

CAPITAL
BOOKS, INC.
Sterling, Virginia

Capital Books, Inc.
P.O. Box 605
Herndon, Virginia 20172-0605

ISBN 1-931868-27-1   (alk. paper)

Library of Congress Cataloging-in-Publication Data

Kelly, Donovan, 1941–
    Quest for the holy grill : 50 crummy but good restaurants within rambling range of Washington, D.C.—1st ed.
        p. cm.
    Includes index.
    ISBN 1–931868–27–1
    1. Restaurants—Washington Region—Guidebooks. I. Title.

TX907.3.W3 K46 2002
647.95753—dc21   2002073307

Printed in the United States of America on acid-free paper that meets the American National Standards Institute Z39-48 Standard.

First Edition

10 9 8 7 6 5 4 3 2 1

This book is dedicated

to the hope that a certain mom will continue to share her well-timed pats on the back and kicks in the tail and that a certain wife who deserves better will remain my constant companion, even on my liver-and-onion days. You two keep bringing on the good and I'll do the crummy.

Contents

CONTENTS

Crummy But Good West and South of the Potomac (cont.)

Crummy But Good East and North of the Potomac   69

CONTENTS

CONTENTS

IN THE BEGINNING:
ANGER AND HARMONY

The Quest, the search for the perfect Crummy But Good (CBG) restaurant, began in anger. Or in Harmony, if you use the old name for Hamilton, VA.

The anger was served up by one of my favorite CBG restaurant owners. Tim O'Neil slammed my smoked-chicken sandwich down on the table in front of me, rattling dust that had lain long undisturbed on the windowsill. A few days before, I had described his restaurant—Planet Wayside—in the *Washington Post* thusly: "It's crummy-looking, but the home-cooked hickory-smoked chicken and barbecue are great and the off-the-wall humor plentiful."

The editor of the *Post's* Food Section made me do it. In the draft of one of my first articles for Nancy McKeon, I had described the joys of picking wild berries in western Loudoun County. I had also foolishly dipped into a mythology of how serious berry pickers in this semirural area, fifty miles west of Washington, DC, protected the secrets of their berry patches. Editor McKeon does not suffer fools or secrets. She asked for a map showing the location of some of the wild patches.

Because such a map would surely get me tarred and feathered by my berry-picking neighbors, I tried to fill the map with anything but secret berry patches. Instead, I showed the location of three of my favorite down-home restaurants, claiming that these were places where all professional wild berry pickers ate.

Restaurant owner Tim O'Neil, his better-than-home-cooking wife, Suzanne, and several of their tougher-looking customers took offense at my comments about the crummy appearance of Planet Wayside. So what if the appearance of the place had gone downhill since serving as an infamous beer garden in the 1930s? "Maybe we crummy-looking restaurants deserve special reviews of our own," Tim snarled at me, almost bouncing smoked chicken into my lap.

I accepted the challenge. And so the Quest for the Holy Grill, the search for the perfect CBG restaurant began. Editor McKeon may not like secrets, but she enjoyed challenging readers of her Food Section, and hundreds of them responded and continue to respond to nominate their own favorite Crummy But Good places. A while after the *Post* series ended, I began doing a monthly segment with David Furst on Metro Connection on WAMU Radio (88.5 FM) in Washington. This brought on another satisfying wave of nominations by a small but dedicated and growing crew of Crummy But Good Scouts who have joined the Quest. With luck, we will never finish the Quest until the world is once more ready and safe for our favorite CBG restaurants. Once more into the greasy breech my friends!

CRUMMY BUT GOOD DEFINED

Except for those who are terminally highbrow, most of us seem to have a natural sense of what is Crummy and what is Good. We also understand that a place can be "Crummy" yet "Good" at the same time. "Crummy" is the immediate knee-jerk reaction to outside appearances, a reaction that might make you cringe, or say "Yuck." "Crummy" is not evil or bad—just the opposite of "elegant" or "hoity-toity." Likewise, the "Good" is a combination of impressions—of feeling at home and of finding tasty food, good menu, reasonable prices, new friends, and maybe something different. You know you've found "Good" when you start thinking about coming back again and maybe bringing your smart aleck brother from New Jersey who thinks he's seen everything. "Good" has nothing to do with "proper" or "being seen" or "cute" and does not dwell in cookie-cutter restaurant chains with faraway owners.

I know most of us share this sense and understanding of Crummy But Good, because hundreds of readers have responded to my articles and continue to send me scouting reports on their favorite CBG places.

Knowing that several of our CBG scouts are also geologists or lawyers, I have set down some totally scientific and legally binding guidelines and definitions:

GRADING: Each restaurant can earn a maximum total of 10 points, 5 CCCCC points for being perfectly "crummy" and five GGGGG points for "but perfectly good" using the following sliding definitions:

CRUMMY: A place that on first appearances looks so bad that you would hesitate to invite your mother inside, especially if she were wearing her good dress. The worse the initial impression, the more yuck points it racks up, the more "C"s it gets.

BUT GOOD: Once inside you find a combination of good things. These might include a good menu with lots of variety, tasty food, relaxing atmosphere, friendly people, reasonable prices, and probably something just a bit different. A place that lets you relax and almost put your feet up. A place where the waiters and waitresses know both how to banter and how to leave you alone, and where you find yourself planning on what you'll order the next time you come.

LOCATION: Within 100 miles of Washington, DC. Maybe 125 miles if they have really good pie. As much as I enjoy receiving the nominations from France, Upstate New York, Texas, Baltimore, and other exotic places, I am trying to focus this first Quest on Washington, DC, and neighboring Virginia and Maryland, with just a dash of West Virginia thrown in to add a slight mountain flavor.

YOU KNOW YOU ARE A CRUMMY BUT GOOD SCOUT IF . . .

If you can answer "yes" to at least five of the following statements and can pass the loyalty test, then, my friend, you are ready to come out of the closet and be an official Crummy But Good Scout.

- You are perfectly happy to eat a whole meal with only a single fork.
- You've never seen a place you wouldn't try.
- You have a flannel shirt or tattoo just like the owner's.
- You look forward to reading your place mat.
- You don't ask what's in the meatloaf.
- You can identify more than two of the stains on your menu.
- You can say "linoleum" without lifting your eyebrows.
- You can eat out for a year without saying "cuisine" or "ambiance."
- You automatically spot the location of trash cans so you can bus your own table.
- You don't give a damn if the food is artistically arranged on the plate or not.

- The waitress can call you "Honey" and you don't feel like you have to protest or burn anything.
- You look forward to the challenge of stuffing napkins under uneven table legs.
- You believe delivery trucks or police cars in the parking lot are sure signs of good food.
- You get a persistent small warm glow that isn't the coffee but the pleasure of kids or grandkids asking to go with you to your favorite CBG.

Above all, a Crummy But Good Scout is loyal. A true CBGer displays great loyalty to a favorite place, despite a possible wart or two. As CBGers, we may be slightly embarrassed by "our" place at times, just as we might squirm in the presence of a strange uncle or a snotty-nosed, not-cool kid brother. But in the end, it's our family, our place, against the world. Take on my place, you take on me. It's us versus them, and we know who we are and we know who they are.

A favorite CBG restaurant becomes a haven and a home turf, the closest we are going to get to the "Cheers" tavern and the "Friends" coffeehouse of TV land. It is an insider's club whose members have paid their dues, overcoming heartburn and grease stains to learn the secrets of what is extra good on the menu and to form a bond of comradeship with those who have served in the CBG trenches with them. Loyal patrons who have earned the right to be greeted extra warmly and to be asked the big badge question of membership: "Do you want your usual?"

THE FUN IS IN THE QUEST

The fun of the Quest for the Holy Grill is in the search. Sure, some lucky ones already have that favorite CBG restaurant, where everyone knows their face and they feel down-home and safe. But the luckiest ones will be those CBG scouts who have found a favorite CBG but still quest on, still search for a far, far better place, the perfect CBG restaurant, the Holy Grill, the perfect CCCCCGGGGG.

And in that search are the stories and legends, the ups and downs, that can keep us laughing and enjoying, despite hearts that burn, stomachs that churn, and plastic forks that break. Our personal Crummy But Good scrapbook that is much more than a rack of fine whines: a well-savored collection of the best and worst of waitresses, perfect pies, and awful gravy, of dumps to avoid and places we can't wait to revisit.

Onward!

TEN BEST

So here I am, reviewing CBG restaurants, my own favorites and those most highly recommended by readers and friends. Might as well jump into the deep impossible end of the CBG pool and try to name the ten best CBG restaurants. Of course, crumminess and goodness are all in the eyes and stomach of the beholder, which is mostly me, with a lot of input from Crummy But Good scouts and reviewing companions. This top ten crummybutgood list thus reflects not only my own favorites but also those places that have generated the most favorable scouting reports. Bear in mind that these are snapshot reviews, subject to change, which is why we stopped quoting prices. With all these disclaimers behind us, if you asked me right now to name my ten favorites, I would pick these:

- Planet Wayside (VA)
- Barbara Fritchie Candlestick Restaurant (MD)
- Ben's Whole Hog Barbecue (VA)
- Bridge Restaurant (MD)
- Cafe Monti (VA)
- Ercilia's Restaurant (DC)
- Havabite Eatery (VA)
- Li Ho Food Restaurant (DC)
- Vienna Inn (VA)
- The Waffle Shop (DC)

REVIEWS OF THE CURRENT TOP TEN

PLANET WAYSIDE

Business Route 7 on the west end of Hamilton, VA, about seven miles west of Leesburg, VA; phone: 540-338-4315.

C C C C G G G G

Original Home of the Crummy But Good

Sorry, Tim, but Planet Wayside remains, by an overwhelming vote, crummy looking.

Yes, the new ceiling paint helps. But I've consulted with many of your patrons, including a poet who won a Pulitzer Prize and another who should have. We all agree that "crummy looking" remains the only appropriate description of what looks like a condemned chicken coop. Weeds jam the wobbly-looking front of the restaurant and reach as high as the narrow windows. Only the big Planet Wayside sign looks new and solid, and already it is starting to lean south. The narrow front door is always stuck, the ceiling too low, and the nonentranceway is dominated inside by a space heater, fuse box, and rickety air conditioner. Four tables and two short counters can allegedly serve twenty-eight people. The overflow goes out back to a patio that is nicely situated among the trees, but where the tables and chairs are subject to the dropping and flying by of unnamed stuff.

And yet, Planet Wayside remains my favorite, my personal CBG restaurant home. Good humor abounds and the food is outstanding. The menu staples of Tim's home-smoked or barbecued chicken, pork, beef, and trout are well above average, and the daily specials and homemade desserts created by wife Suzanne push the Wayside into Crummy Nirvana.

On one visit, the specials included crabcake sandwiches and Tijuana grill. The Tijuana grill was two thick slices of homemade bread grilled with a yummy, zingy mixture of chicken, sun dried tomatoes, mountain jack cheese, green chili peppers, chopped scallions, and a dressing, plus other ingredients I couldn't identify but enjoyed. The grill also included a cold white bean and tomato salad. That same day, there were at least eight homemade desserts available: five pies (from peach to chocolate coffee crunch), multifruit cobbler, cheesecake, and macadamia fudge cake.

If the food doesn't get you, the humor will. Outside, Tim has created a local tourist attraction on sleepy Business Route 7 with daily zany messages on a blackboard: "Brain Dead Served Here"; "Tonight's Event: Midget Mud Wrestling on Prozac"; "Free Broken Appliances, the Perfect West Virginia Lawn Ornaments." Inside are the usual warning signs: "Unattended Children Will Be Sold As Slaves." And Tim

O'Neil himself is even worse. Maybe it's good he's not speaking to me, just as long as I'm allowed to keep eating the good food at his crummy-looking restaurant.

BARBARA FRITCHIE CANDYSTICK RESTAURANT

U.S. 40 on the western edge of Frederick, MD; phone: 301-662-2500.

C C G G G

Brer Rabbit and Pie Heaven

Just when everything was feeling satisfactual, Brer Rabbit starts having a bad mouth day. His teeth begin to curdle and his tongue tastes like snails and stink bugs had been crawling all around.

First Fan Jane Perry (Herndon, VA) said what Brer Rabbit needed was a good dose of Barbara Fritchie Candystick Restaurant. "No, no!" said Brer Rabbit. "Not Barbara Fritchie! I'm not dragging this sorry cottontail all the way to Frederick, MD, up confusanating Route 40 and past all those tree-bare shopping malls."

But Sister Jane insisted: "The pies are outstanding. And it's my sixteen-year-old son Rodger's favorite place."

"No, no!" said Brer Rabbit. " I'm not going near that ticky-tack restaurant with its sorry candy cane standing in front. It looks like a poor pale step-cousin of a failed Howard Johnson's. Their proudest thing is a bunch of cheap-looking plastic lights that Denmark threw away forty years ago."

But a First Fan is a First Fan, and Sister Jane, she just threw that rabbit right into the Fritchie briar patch. Brer Rabbit kicked and hollered like the snails and stinkbugs had started acrawlin' in his mouth again. But soon the old rabbit got real quiet. And then he said, his mouth just a drippin' with the happys, "I fooled you. Been coming to Barbara Fritchie for thirty years. Only thing better than the roast pork sandwich (with real potatoes, real gravy, and sassy pepper slaw) and the barbecue platter (with potato salad and pepper slaw) are the pies. For this rabbit, it's pie heaven, baked daily."

Now maybe you don't believe in no talking rabbits with visions of pie heaven. But waitresses Nancy and Helen, they been in that Fritchie patch even longer than me. And when they see this rabbit coming, they lock up the pie safe extra good. You just asks them if that's not true. (Forgive me and thank you Uncle R.)

Another long-memoried fan, Ken Briers (Washington, DC) reminds us that the Barbara Fritchie business "was originally located downtown, near the still-standing original Barbara Fritchie House, selling candy to the tourists who stopped there when U.S. Route 40 passed through town on Patrick Street. As a child growing up in Baltimore, my family made regular trips through Frederick to visit relatives in Southwest Pennsylvania. One of our games was to count the endless parade of signs for Barbara Fritchie Candy that were visible for miles, in both directions."

And hence the tacky candy cane sign and the word "CANDY" in big bold letters that still stand in front of the restaurant. Although Fritchie stopped making chocolates about twenty years ago, the lingering outside emphasis on CANDY seems to discourage some parents from stopping, the same dedicated parents who seek sugar-free checkout lanes at the grocery store. Good. Because that leaves more of Fritchie great home cooking for the rest of us.

Shoot, better than home cooking. What home makes fresh pies daily, not to mention fresh roast turkey, roast pork, chicken pot pies, and real potatoes mashed and French fried? What other restaurant brags about legendary local heroine Barbara Fritchie and then hides her ugly picture outside the restrooms? Where else can an early bird get fresh sugared fastnachts with real trucker coffee?

Please don't tell our favorite waitress, Helen, that the place has gotten a little worn down and for sure don't use the "C" word as in Crummy. After forty years, she's a bit protective. Rumors have a new owner coming who has promised not to change anything. But just in case, you might want to visit the Barbara Fritchie Candystick Restaurant soon.

BEN'S WHOLE HOG BARBECUE

7422 Old Centreville Road, Manassas, VA;
phone: 703-331-5980; fax: 703-331-2142.
C C C G G G G

Clod Finds Clod

"This is where the Little Sisters of the Poor would hold their convention," my rookie crummybutgood scouting companion said as we entered the restaurant.

I'm not sure what that means either, but his words felt right. The outside of Ben's Whole Hog Barbecue wouldn't draw sinners and the inside feels monastery bleak, just a large, almost cavernous dining area perfect for feeding huddled masses. Except no soup kitchen ever smelled so good.

The centerpiece on our first visit was a whole hog stretched out on the counter, sizzling hot out of one of the huge brick indoor ovens that Ben had built himself. Ben stood proudly over the hog, not saying a word, just admiring his work. I joined the admiring circle and couldn't resist sneaking a taste when Ben offered. Outstanding and not in need of any of the three sauces available.

Ben's was by far the favorite place among CBG scouts who voted in the First Barbecue Quest, possibly aided by a bit of Internet support that drew e-mail from fans as far away as Charlotte, NC. The pulled BBQ pork platter at Ben's was delicious and obviously fresh, and the side dishes were well above average, especially the homemade coleslaw, BBQ beans, and sweet potato soufflé.

But wait. Ben has since added a beef shoulder clod to the menu that is the best barbecued beef I have tasted yet. The clod is a boneless center cut that comes in twenty-five-pound roasts that Ben cooks over oak and hickory for seventeen hours. He has also added a groaning board all-you-can-eat buffet, at very reasonable lunch, early bird, and dinner prices that would be illegal in six right-to-eat states. On weekends and some weekday nights, there is live music without a cover charge featuring area singers and bands. Bring lots of cholesterol medication, stretch pants, and your foot-stomping shoes.

Because barbecue can be the perfect take-out food, I try to test the travelability of the offerings at each restaurant. At Ben's the beef clod, pulled pork, and smoked turkey (all available by the pound) proved exceptionally fine fellow travelers that lost little in reheating.

I did subtract a point from Ben's final score for the lackluster desserts. As if they mattered. If we had room for dessert, we would have just eaten more barbecue. My rookie dining companion insisted the pie was worth two plus points, but he also tried to take away two points because Ben's parking lot was paved and not a proper redneck gravel lot where he could spin his truck tires. I sent him down to the crummybutgood scouting farm team for rehabilitation.

BRIDGE RESTAURANT

On the Hancock, MD, side of the Route 522 bridge over the Potomac River; serves breakfast seven days a week, and on the right Saturday mornings, live old-time music; no phone available.
CCCGGG

A Musical Bridge

The thing is, my dad has been dead for almost twenty years. So I really didn't expect to hear him singing when I opened the door of the Bridge Restaurant.

We really didn't expect to hear anyone singing. Who sings at breakfast time in a little old down-home country restaurant? My wife and I were still in our morning fog, still in desperate need of that second cup of coffee. Comfortable spouses, in that morning time of barely talking let alone singing. Just twenty miles into a three hundred-mile trip back home to Pennsylvania. All we wanted was a quick breakfast. This one lasted almost two hours and we loved every minute.

We did notice that the small parking lot was full at the restaurant, but we were completely surprised by the live music that spilled out as we opened the door:

Come and sit by my side if you love me,
Do not hasten to bid me adieu.

It wasn't really Dad singing. Just three older gentlemen with guitars and banjo ("Sam" Sammons, Tom Sexton, and Paige Heston) singing my dad's songs, the songs of the 20s and 30s.

> Five foot two, eyes of blue
> Could she, could she, cootchy coo,
> Has anybody seen my girl?

The waitress/wife/co-owner, Frances Younker, poured our coffee and took our orders. Then she said, in the voice of busy mothers everywhere, "The coffeepot will be over there on the end of the counter if you need more. Donuts too. Help yourselves." She left to get her favorite gospel songbook and joined the cook/husband/co-owner, Lowell Younker, in leading the next song:

> Just a closer walk with thee,
> Jesus grant my humble plea.

Dad loved to sing the old hymns in church. When the hymnbooks came out, he would slide down the pew a bit to get away from those members of his family who were tone deaf—namely me. For awhile I thought he just wanted more room to belt out the chorus. I would raise my voice to fill the increased pew space between us—until Mom gently suggested that perhaps some people are meant to be hummers, not singers.

When Dad sang "Oh Donny Boy" then I knew for sure that all was right with the world:

> Oh, Donny Boy, the pipes . . . . the pipes are calling,
> From glen to glen and down the mountain side.
> The summer's gone and all the leaves are falling,
> Tis you, Tis you must go and I must bide.

(As sung at the Bridge ever so sweetly by Margie Sweet.)
  Don't try to tell me it's really "Oh Danny Boy." I grew up

knowing it was "Oh Donny Boy," Dad's special song to me, his son Don, to assure me that I had been forgiven for all past pranks. And that's the way I'll hum it now.

On the road back home, we stopped at the Bridge Restaurant. Instead of a quick breakfast, we found a musical bridge between then and now. And with the last sip of coffee, I left my thanks for being allowed to hear Dad sing again.

(PS: They serve breakfast only from 7 to 11 A.M., seven days a week. I recommend the country ham and eggs on a Saturday morning and just hope the old guys feel like playing that day.)

CAFE MONTI

**3250 Duke Street, Alexandria, VA;
phone: 703-370-3632.**
C C G G G G

Ask Not for Whom the Kraut is Sauer

I would hit a bad sauerkraut day. Not bad, actually, just not real sauer. But who am I to comment on Austrian food? Austrian cooking remains one of the three thousand national and regional foods that I do not claim to be an expert in. I only know crummy and good. Cafe Monti is definitely good with just the right dash of crummy.

Not the down-and-dirty crummy of indifference or greasy overindulgence in fried food, but the calculated crummy of good food first, fast and right, and we'll worry about looking pretty later. For now, enjoy the view of the soft drink coolers and don't forget to bus your own tables.

That's assuming you can get a table. At lunchtime on our first visit, all tables belonged to the quick-footed. Slow-footed optimists like us ordered our food at the take-out counter and hung out around the edges, a small circle of table wolves ready to pounce at the first sign of a napkin being crumpled or of a hand reaching for a coat.

First Fan Diane Atkins (Sterling, VA) "discovered" Cafe Monti in the traditional way: her husband works next door at Mattress Discounters. Second Fan Helen Schmid (Washington, DC) wrote in praise of the daily specials. "The mussels marinara with pasta are as good as any place in the city, and for a lot less money."

We enjoyed our specials. My companion reported that his penne with eggplant, in a fresh tomato and garlic sauce, "was really quite nice." (He's just a country boy, but he talks like that when he gets into the big city.)

My smoked pork chops with sauerkraut and fried potatoes seemed undersauered. Confessing my ignorance, I asked former owner and cook Vic Kreidl if Austrian food was less sauer than German. I had to wait patiently for an answer while a well-dressed woman gave him a kiss with her take-out order. Obviously a well-pleased customer. "No, no. But American sauerkraut is too sour. I have to wash it. And today, maybe, it is not sour enough," Vic said.

On later visits, Vic had left and new owners taken over. They have assured me that the menu has not changed, and so far they have been right. Good daily specials and lunch and dinner menus that range from steak and cheese subs through a range of pastas, from Austrian goulash to homemade cannoli and strudel. Now we have another CBG excuse to explore Duke Street.

ERCILIA'S RESTAURANT

3070 Mount Pleasant Street NW, Washington, DC; phone: 202-387-0909.

C C C C G G G G

From Fresh Dough Fat Tortillas Grow

"Good sign. They're using fresh dough in the kitchen," my expert on all things Latin American whispered to me. And that is exactly why I had asked him to join me.

I was too nervous eyeing the fifty-item Spanish menu to spot something like fresh dough. The menu was hand lettered (with English subtitles) and hung over the head of the cashier. She was also one of the three food servers stuffed into the tiny kitchen. I could feel the line of impatient customers growing behind me. I was trying so hard not to look like a clueless gringo tourist while struggling to remember my high school Spanish that I ignored the fresh dough being turned into Salvadoran tortillas.

Straight line: What's the difference between a Salvadoran tortilla and a Mexican tortilla?

Punch line: The same as the difference between a hamburger and a tofu-burger: fatter, greasier, and tastier.

Bottom line: "Better food than any home cooking I've had in South America," my expert guide said. His clueless gringo sidekick (me) was equally impressed.

First Fan Bettie Kahn (Washington, DC) said, "It may be self-serve and paper plates (C), but it's also fresh, tasty, friendly, and cheap (G)." When Bettie is right, she's right. Even the hongos that came with my pollo were fresh (chicken with mushrooms, fat tortillas, refried beans, and feta-like cheese). My companion was equally pleased with the tomatoes, which he was sure were ripened on the vine just before they joined his plato guanaco (includes pupusas—described as the Salvadoran national dish, a pork and cheese filling stuffed inside a thick soft tortilla and fried on the grill—with refried beans and a tomato relish/salad).

Another fan, Andrea Louise Heggen (Arlington, VA), once lived in Mount Pleasant and remembers, "Before it was a restaurant, Ercilia's was a big truck with propane-fired cookers, parked on Mt. Pleasant Street near Rat Park and the junction of 16th, Mt. Pleasant, and Harvard Streets. My daughter and I used to stop often for pupusas and tacos." A truck from Ercilia's still works the construction sites, but now we don't have to track it down.

In the absence of a wine list, I selected from the cooler a fine brown Inca Cola that was very not dry. My companion tried a can of even sweeter red watermelon soft drink labeled "soda aromatise a la Pasteque." I had no idea what it meant. Thus, I remained to the end, a happy clueless gringo in the land of fat tortillas that tofu forgot.

HAVABITE EATERY

10416 Main Street, Fairfax, VA; phone: 703-591-2244.
C C G G G

Mousaka by Any Other Name

Still I get this comment from would-be Crummy But Good scouts. "I hesitate to recommend my favorite place to you because I don't really want them to be considered 'crummy'—it is a wonderful small restaurant for good home cooking and friendly atmosphere," said Patricia Levine (Fairfax City, VA).

It's Okay, Patricia. We say "Crummy" with a lot of love, as in "You old coot you" or "You're really bad." It's just a warning that this place might not be as plastic slick as your favorite hamburger chain or as floppydo elegant as the place you take a date to impress her with stiff waiters and soft napkins.

And you're right, Patricia. Havabite is a CBG down-home keeper. "Red-checked oilcloth tablecloths, pictures colored by kids taped to the wall, and a kitchen so small that only the two thin cooks can fit into it."

We found the place packed with regulars of all kinds—suits to blue jeans—at noon and then suddenly empty at 1:20. As if a bell had rung at nearby Fairfax Court House and recess was over. Despite the crowd, the owner let our table yak on long after our dishes were cleared. Just long enough for me to get a parking ticket. Hmm. Maybe there is a conspiracy between restaurant and Court House.

Naw, no way. Pop Havabite (aka Harry Dmetriou) wouldn't do that to us. We definitely felt at home. Including the good-natured kid brother starring as the waiter who hadn't yet tried the food himself on the Greek-Italian side of the menu. But I cannot resist mousaka. It was the point-to-it-in-the-taberna-kitchen food of choice on our honeymoon in Greece, back when mousaka was really mousaka and so was I.

Our tall companion met his first spanakopita (spinach and feta cheese wrapped in flaky filo dough). He became an instant filophyte, which is now legal in Virginia. The other companion, who wanted to be called witty, rated his souvlaki "good, but not exceptional."

First Fan Patricia said, "We eat there every Friday night when we are in town, and usually have the steak and cheese sandwich, the best anywhere—including Atlantic City or Philadelphia." Challenge noted.

Second Fan Carol Kaltenbaugh said, "It has been our favorite little place for fifteen years. I love their grilled Swiss sandwiches, their Greek soup, and the marinated chicken over rice is superb—and heats up great at home."

As we left, our would-be-witty companion pointed out the clogged rain gutters with grass growing in them. And he made me add a "C" to our review because there were too many lawyer-like people in the restaurant. Maybe he would be more fun if he ate more mousaka.

Li Ho Food Restaurant

501 H Street NW, Washington, DC;
phone: 202-289-2059.
C C C C G G G

Singapore Noodle and the Case of the Pink Slip

She said I'd find happiness on a street named H in a town called China. A town of a hundred cheap chopstick joints hidden in a city with a thousand cheap things to hide.

Me, I'm just a rube with a fork. I needed a chopstick guide. I found him, but I wasn't ready for the pink slip. This is the story.

My guide took me to Li Ho's place. Not sure I wanted to go in. Something about the bright red and yellow grimy face of the place said it was tougher than me. Yellow scars of paper flapped in the window, clippings that bragged about being the best cheap restaurant in 1984. Inside was even tougher. I tried to ignore the decorations: hanging ducks and chickens. Whatever their crime, these birds were doing their time the hard way. Beyond the poultry curtain, a back table of off-duty kitchen help made authentic Chinese background noises. My eyes slowly adjusted to the new pink paint over the fake wood paneling. Paint that needed to fade. Fast.

The waiter stared past me, gave my guide a big grin and greeted him warmly by his Chinatown name, "Singapore Noodle"?

Whatever his real name, we came for the food. First Fan Cathy Wine (Washington, DC) wrote in a hurry, on the back of a faded flyer, "The decor is definitely crummy, but it is our favorite Chinese restaurant, especially the chow foon and the eggplant with garlic."

The street name for chow mai foon is Singapore noodle. The same as my guide. He confessed to being a Li Ho addict. A soft noodle, just crispy enough, just curried enough. That's my guide. The chow mai foon too.

We also did the eggplant with garlic. It was that kind of lunch. Lots. Good. The warning spice stars on the menu were just for rubes.

I took the food bill as I sipped the last of the hot, earthy tea. "What kind of tea is this?" I asked the waiter. I cleared my ears for a long Chinese name. "Red tea," said the waiter.

I had to make him talk. It's my job. Under the food bill was a pink slip of paper, folded and carefully taped to the plate. I showed it to my guide. He shrugged. "It's always there. The first time I opened it. I thought the waitress had left me her phone number. But it was blank."

I turned to grill the waiter. "What is this?" I said, pointing to the pink slip of folded paper. He looked at me hard and said, "It is nothing." And walked away.

Chinatown is like that. The east wind blows bits of inscrutable down H Street and you learn not to ask.

VIENNA INN

120 Maple Avenue East, Vienna, VA;
phone: 703-938-9548.
C C C G G G

Double Dog with Chili and Tears, Hold the Insults

A lot of people rave about the Vienna Inn. I don't. In deference to my physical safety, let me restate my position. A lot of very large geologists and, I'm told, although I have no need to know, members of the CIA love the place. They write me every month. My house is being watched. Strange people carrying rock hammers appear at my door.

So, I recommend the Vienna Inn. Now can I have my son back?

When I'm in the mood for two good chili dogs with onions, a cold beer, and loud conversation with geologists and spies, this is where I head. Any place that can boast that it serves a ton of hot dogs every month and that its chief cook was trained at the Culinary Institute of America should do at least one thing—chili dogs—extremely well. And the Vienna Inn does.

If you have a Ralph Nadering dislike of hot dogs, First Fans Patti Tuholski and Jan Arneson suggest trying the Chili Mac (spaghetti topped with chili, cheese, and onions).

Perhaps the main attraction is Molly, the hostess with the mostest gravel in her voice and the quickest edge on her tongue. A tongue so sharp it should be registered as a lethal weapon. But you tell her. I'm not going to. After Molly yelled at me, I found myself sitting very straight, keeping my elbows off the table, and promising to eat all my broccoli. Fortunately, the Vienna Inn is definitely a broccoli-and-tofu-free zone, which is the second best thing about the place. A CIA informant carrying a rock hammer recently tried to tell me that Molly has mellowed and doesn't come around so much anymore, but I think it's just a trick to get me back.

THE WAFFLE SHOP

522 10th Street NW, across from Ford's Theater, Washington, DC; phone: 202-638-3430.
C C C G G G G

The Waffle Shop That's Also Not

Legend has it that President Lincoln really wanted to dine here that bad night, but the Mrs. refused to sit on stools that swivel, so they went to the theater across the street instead.

Several fans disagree with Mrs. Lincoln. "The place has three U-shaped counters, circa 1940, with very comfortable well-seasoned oak stools that both swivel and have a back rest, much appreciated by the beleaguered federal worker," said First Fan Mike Walker (Washington, DC).

A Faraway Fan (D. J. Janik, Denver, CO) has cased the joint well: "As a law-enforcement professional, whenever I'm in DC, I seek out and revel in the stark, no-nonsense setting . . . and seasoned Formica . . . an oasis of simplicity and sincerity in a world run amok with restaurant themes, faux decor, and rampant pretension."

I arrived expecting the Waffle Shop to be a waffle shop, only to find that the restaurant also specializes in Chinese-American food. My companion immediately ordered Chinese (combination lomein with shrimp, chicken, and beef) and declared the noodles pleasantly fresh. Stubbornly sticking to the waffle motif, I ordered the waffle breakfast special (waffle, two jumbo eggs, ham, bacon, sausages or scrapple, coffee or tea). Then I pushed my luck and tested the sign that said "Breakfast Served All Day Long." I also ordered grits.

"We're out of grits," the cook said gruffly, taking a long look at the clock. Okay, it was 2:30 in the afternoon, a time when all good grits are either long gone or long overcooked. But the waffle was crisp and fresh and the homefries a reasonable alternative.

Mrs. Lincoln, you really made a mistake.

CRUMMY BUT GOOD WEST AND SOUTH OF THE POTOMAC

ARLINGTON AND FAIRFAX COUNTIES

ANGIE'S FAMILY RESTAURANT

Twinbrooke Shopping Center, 9569 Braddock Road, Fairfax, VA; phone: 703-978-5518.
C G G G

Angie's without Angie

Just don't ask for Angie at Angie's. Because Angie doesn't live here anymore. She's been back home in Greece for about ten years now. Her look-alike younger sister Elles lets people call her "Angie," but even her patience does have a limit. Elles came in "just to help out a little" nineteen years ago and sometimes wonders why she's not back in Greece herself, "where things are a little bit slower."

Her service wasn't slow. It was fast, friendly, and as full of banter as we wanted. A nice way to ease into Saturday morning. Companion A did note that his French toast (two pieces with sausage or bacon) carried a hint of the same onion and spices as the home fries and western omelet (with toast or biscuit) ordered by companion B. Perhaps their orders shared the same grill or perhaps Greek French toast is meant to be spicier than Mom's.

Companion B fought for my grits, but lost. My Angie's Special (two eggs, two pancakes, sausage or bacon, toast or biscuit) came as I ordered, with my eggs over easy and ready to run with the grits, while carefully avoiding Mr. Pancake and his lake of syrup. Ah, perfect Saturday morning breakfast harmony: everyone together, mixing it up a little bit, but carefully not crossing those final serious frontiers.

Second Fan Chuck McKeon (Fairfax, VA) said we would be making a big mistake if we didn't try the pizza. What makes it different from all the other pizzas around? "The number of people required to lift it!" Fan Chuck said. "And the value—good, but cheap. A large Angie's Special has lots of everything, including cheese. Angie's husband, Arthur, used to put Coke in the dough. The result is a thick, but airy, somewhat sweet crust. The current chef seems to follow the 'original' recipe."

First Fan Pat Nash also praised the evening menu. "We've heard the pizza is good, but we always have the souvlaki—either the sandwich with a side of wonderful fries, or the platter, which comes with a Greek salad."

Fan Pat should know. She's been going to Angie's for at least fifteen years and rates the decor as both "interesting and a bit tacky. We do so miss the silver metallic bamboo-themed wallpaper that was in place for years and years."

Who can forget the good old days of Angie and the silver bamboo? But at least we had Elles. She and the duct tape on the seats made us feel right at home. The latest follow-up review by scouts Karole and Diehl McKalip reported things a bit less crummy and new owners, second cousins to the previous owners, they think, so hopefully everything will remain in the Angie family way of doing good with just a pleasant touch of crummy.

WHITEY'S RESTAURANT

2761 N. Washington Blvd., Arlington, VA; phone: 703-525-9825; www.whiteyseat.com. C C C G G G

Grillstoned, Deer Reared, and Belated

Dear Mrs. Rae Phillips,

In 1998 you were very right. You wrote to remind me—apparently for the second time—that Whitey's is "such a perfect place for your Crummy But Good column."

Somehow your letter got very misplaced and I did not find it until February 2002. The very next day I visited Whitey's and had a belated great time.

No, I didn't take advantage of the pool table in the back or the coin-operated steam shovel machine in the corner of the cavernous dining room. Owner Calvin Seville had to point out that I was sitting directly below the stuffed hindquarter of a deer, whose head was mounted on the other side of the wall, facing the bar.

To be honest, I didn't really like my platter of the house specialty, "broasted" chicken. Just too extra crisp and chewy for me, like chicken jerky, although a lot of people around me were obviously enjoying theirs. And since I was working, I also did not try any of the twelve draft beers or seven wines available by the glass.

No, Mrs. Phillips, what I really liked is something added since you wrote—Stonegrill dining. This is a platter with two pockets on the side and a slab of superheated "volcanic granite" in the middle. Superheated as in 750 degrees hot when it leaves the special oven and designed to stay above 350 degrees for forty-five minutes while you grill your meat, fish or poultry just the way you like it. Talk about a natural conversation piece and icebreaker on a cold date. This is what I needed when I was young and tongue-tied and used to be King of the Nerds. And whenever I remind people that I used to be King of the Nerds, my son always replies, "what do you mean, 'used to be'?"

Mrs. Linda kept warning me that I was grilling my steak too long if I wanted it medium rare. Leave me alone! Can't you see I'm playing with my food!

Okay, if your mommy won't let you play with your food or you have young children who should be nowhere near a slab of superhot granite, then there are plenty of other menu items to pick from. If you're on a tight budget, there is some sort of special drink or food every night, including half-price burger day, that almost forces you to eat out. Many nights feature live music and Happy Hour strikes often.

So what if the edges look rough, the heating pipes glisten, and the seats lean and sag? Fifty years will do that to you. Where else can you sit under a deer's rear end in complete safety? Try Whitey's. Mrs. Phillips said so. And don't wait four years like I did.

CELEBRITY DELLY

Loehmann's Plaza, 7263-A Arlington Boulevard, Falls Church, VA; phone: 703-573-9002.
C C G G G

Raising a Deli-cate Question

It said so right up front in neon lights: "New York City Deli." Neon wouldn't lie, would it? Because what do I know from a New York City deli? On my few visits to delicatessens in New York, I remember strange treats like herring mixed with crowded loudness and a freedom, if not a requirement, to shout. A rudeness shared like dark mustard, sharp and essential. All this the Celebrity Delly can do, in a slightly decaffeinated way. But could it ever pass as a real New York deli?

Fortunately, my extensive volunteer scouting staff includes a New York City deli expert, reared in the Bronx, where he squandered his allowance playing the delicatessens during World War II. "My mother would give me fifty cents and I'd get a corned beef sandwich, a Coke and French fries," Mr. Bronx said. So I lent him fifty cents and we headed for Celebrity Delly.

He stopped me at the door and pointed to the first troubling sign—Lite Cream Cheese. "Probably not kosher. Can't mix dairy and meats. Must be one of those accommodating dellys," he said with a sigh. But he approved of the bustling noon crowd and the shouting and joking between patrons and staff. "This feels right." While we waited for a table for three, we helped direct timid twosomes to tables they could share with other couples.

The bill for my expert's fifty-cent special of corned beef sandwich, French fries, and a Coke was about eighteen-times over budget. Mr. Bronx pronounced the corned beef good, although the staff had no idea what he was talking about when he tried to order a single-breasted corned beef—the top cut without the fat and gristle that's in a double-breasted corned beef.

He also approved of my creamed herring (with onions, cucumbers, tomato, pickles, bagel, and cream cheese). Of course, by Bronx standards, the pickles were only half sour and should be a darker green, as they would be if they had spent more time meditating in a wooden barrel.

From the more than sixty sandwiches and submarines listed, our third companion ordered a tuna melt. He reported that his tuna had mostly migrated to the downstream half of his sandwich. "I guess it's okay," he said. Myself, I can't imagine any tuna melt sandwich ever rating higher than an okay. Especially when surrounded by options like the New Yorker sandwich, which includes a two-meal supply of pastrami and kosher dog covered with melted cheese, coleslaw, and Russian dressing on grilled rye bread.

I asked the manager how much New York City deli experience he actually had. "Well, I've been to some Broadway musicals," he said. "But I have a lot of Falls Church deli experience." Good enough for us.

Satisfied with his meal, my expert decided to take something special home to his New York wife. After looking over the menu and all the bakery selections, he selected a romantic pound of chopped liver.

At last, the perfect crummybutgood gift for that special someone. Say it with chopped liver.

PEPPER'S TEXAS BAR-B-Q

1810 Michael Faraday Drive, in an office park off Sunset Hills Drive, Reston, VA; phone: 703-435-9696. C C G G

Token Old Texas Crummy in a New Town

Reston was created in a spirit of something for everyone, and Pepper's Texas Bar-B-Q is the New Town's token crummy place. A dark space where everyone can forget their place in the office pecking order. Where A-drive bosses in stiff suits can relax with coworkers over lunch. Where you can pretend you are way back home, far from here and the only Beltway involves taking a belt with a long-necked beer and a bump.

And if you swallow all that, the sandwiches will taste good. But if it takes more than Texas license plates on the wall to make your Texas barbecue real, well, this dog won't hunt for everyone. I'm three jalapeños short of being a hot-sauce fan, but at Pepper's even I reached for the fire bottle to add life to my barbecue pork sandwich. Our anonymous First Fan praised the meats and sauces—"the beef ribs are big, meaty, and well-cooked." But our Fan also lamented the demise of the flagship location on Route 50 in Fairfax, which "was full service and much nicer."

The cafeteria-style server-cook said that the favorite food is the BBQ beef or pork sandwich with coleslaw, potato chips, and a pickle. "Nobody orders anything else." My companion discovered why when his unlisted, precooked hamburger tasted like new-bride meatloaf. "But it's a great vehicle for the barbecue sauce," he said, loosening his tie and slowly shifting into non A-drive.

QUARTERDECK RESTAURANT
1200 Fort Meyer Drive, Arlington, VA;
phone: 703-528-CRAB (2722).
C C C G G G

Arlington's Cure for the Common Crab

Some days you just feel crabby. Other days you just crave crabs. Nothing fancy, nothing far away. A nearby neighborhood place where you can sit outside, shoot the bull, pick at crabs, drink something cold, and bet on which of the

bug-trapping jars will catch the most bees or yellow jackets. Scratch if you must. So what if your metal table is rusty?

First Fan Phil Million (Arlington, VA) is a man of few words: "Relaxed place! Good softshell crab sandwich at a decent price. Try it!" So we did. One of our dining companions has been going to the Quarterdeck for about twenty-five years. "For the crabs," she said. "And sometimes for the grilled mesquite shrimp. But mostly for my husband, a master picker and teacher of crab picking."

Unfortunately, this turned into a nonpicking lunch day. One of those days when you can only shout, "ARRgh!" A day when the boss ruins your plans for a long, leisurely crab-picking lunch by announcing a sudden one o'clock meeting. Delicious but smelly crabs, unlike oysters, cannot be eaten on days or months with ARRghs in them.

So we cast aside our crab picks and asked the crab gods to bless and keep our bosses—far and farther away from us.

My second choice, the crab cake sandwich platter (with choice of two side dishes, such as coleslaw and potato salad) was okay. Not the big chunks of fresh crabmeat that I look for on the Chesapeake Shore, but more of the filler and frozen taste that creeps into crab cakes as one travels west from the Bay. This was sort of a half-west crab cake.

Our twenty-five-year veteran ventured into the land of fish fillet sandwich and found it satisfactory. "They have learned how to fry without being greasy." But I could see in her eyes the sad longing for crabs not picked.

My younger companions assured me that on Friday and Saturday nights the Quarterdeck is packed with swinging singles. Since I am no longer licensed to practice in either area, I took their word that this was worth another "G" in our review.

(Psst. If you bet on the bug jars, pick the ones baited with ginger ale. They always draw more stinging bees and yellow jackets than the beer-breath jar. Yet another reason to drink beer with your crabs, on those lovely days without ARRghs, when the boss is far, far away.)

SHAMSHIRY CHELO KABOB

8607 Westwood Center Drive, Vienna, VA, west of Tysons Corner off route 7, and just east of the Dulles toll road exit; phone: 703-448-8883.
C G G G G

Schlemiel Meets Shamshiry

Just call me a schlemiel. Or is it schlimazel? Whatever. It's all Moby Dick's fault.

Call me a sucker who can't live up to his own crummy standards whenever a First Fan writes passionately about a favorite CBG restaurant. A slew of readers gently dumped PC (Persian Correct) soup on me after reading how I fumbled the name of the bread oven in a previously written review of Moby Dick's Persian restaurant (Washington, DC). Shall we call the bread

oven in Moby Dick's a tanoor, a tandoor, or just Ishmael? But leave it to Ted Preisser to issue the typical challenge of a good CBG scout defending his own:

"I agree Moby Dick is pretty good, and a pretty good value. But it is not as good as the food at Shamshiry . . . The portions are better, the food is better, and the atmosphere is better. It's Persians cooking Persian food, not Afghanis cooking Persian food. My wife and I lived in Iran, and we say Shamshiry is the best Persian food around."

First Fan Preisser may be right. But Shamshiry isn't very crummy. Do I dare lower my high crummy standards to include a place that just doesn't appear exactly crummy?

But those good "Gs" surely did come through. My companion and I were particularly taken—and taken in—by the Chelo Kabob Shamshiry. We figured out the chelo (rice) part. But the combination of Kabob Kubideh and Kabob Barg had us guessing: was it a combination of beef and lamb or beef and veal?

Wrong. Maybe we lost our keen sense of crummy taste by dipping too deeply into the opening course of green nameless but hot relish dip. We were soon wolfing down bread trying to smother the Persian fire. The panir (goat's cheese) appetizer brought peace to our tongue. Meanwhile we kabobbled the ball on the main course. And if you smugly identify both kabobs correctly on the first bites, I don't want to hear about it.

At busy lunchtime, the place does have the feel of a cafeteria with crowded rectangular tables and minimalist decor, but this was easily offset by the proud fiery look of our waiter and his kind patience in explaining the food in front of us. After watching us struggle, he mixed our masti-khian yogurt appetizer with the mysterious green sauce and joined us in spreading the mix on pieces of the thin bread.

Perhaps the crummiest thing on the menu is the back-page translation of the poem by Omar Khayyam that takes the old love line "A jug of wine, a loaf of bread and thou" and adds a "thigh of mutton." The translation may be Persian Correct, but a "thigh of mutton" sure rates crummy on my romantic scale.

A TASTE OF THE WORLD

283 Sunset Park Drive, Sunset Business Park, near the intersection of Spring Street and Fairfax County Parkway, Herndon, VA; phone: 703-471-2017. C C G G G

Taste the World and Mom's Pies Too

"You should order early. There is trouble in the kitchen," our waiter warned us earnestly on his third visit to our table.

We had been talking and joking while wandering through the extensive lunch menu. Who would do Thai food and who was in an Indian or a Mexican mood? Despite the urgent warning of our waiter, we could see no trouble in the kitchen. Saw no smoke, heard no fighting. Was the vegetarian cook arguing in soft tofu time with the hot-tempered curried chicken cook? More likely, the suddenly full house that was adding to the international flavor was also about to swamp the kitchen with orders. Always listen to your waiter's third warning. We immediately ordered a belated early.

My pad Thai was good, a melting pot of textures. The bean sprouts supplied crisp, the chopped peanuts added crunch, and the noodles and strips of egg omelet offered different softs (chicken, pork, beef, or vegetarian).

First Fan Jack Fischer (St. Michaels, MD) said that the chicken burritos (in a flour tortilla with black beans, rice, lettuce, and tomatoes) "are better than some of the popular local Mexican restaurants make. And to this old sea dog, the smile of the waitress was as warm and welcome as the sun breaking through unexpectedly in the midst of a fierce New England winter squall." Sounds like another case of the Old Man and the CBG.

One of my companions had been a bit reluctant to go into the World. He glanced in disdain at the bright orange and blue interior walls. "They would make a great screen saver for my computer," he said. He ordered a meal-size bowl of won-ton soup (dumplings filled with chicken and chopped water chestnuts in broth). After one last negative comment—"the noodles look like some sort of deep-sea creatures"—Mr. Reluctant quietly ate everything in the whole swimming-pool-size bowl.

The restaurant can be hard to find, tucked away in a business park on the edge of the Fairfax County Parkway, just beyond a series of stark, garage-like buildings. But there is a definite bonus. You also have to pass right by Mom's Apple Pie Company. "You have to stop," said First Fan Mitch Snow. We took turns holding a gun to each other's head.

Of course, it would be very rude and very foolish not to stop and visit Mom's. For purely scientific reasons, I have tried to taste all two dozen varieties of pies they bake—from apple and butter pecan apple crumb to sweet potato and mincemeat. But my selfless systematic pursuit of pie knowledge is constantly side-tracked by random racks of bargain "expired" pies. These are pies that are a few days past their peak quality. Such no-longer-young pies must, of course, be eaten quickly, while the blessings of the God of Frugality make you feel somehow noble and wise.

I will not mention the even cheaper expired pies that have been frozen. That is a secret best kept for the dreary days when taxes come due and you can't possibly afford to eat out ever again.

THELMA'S HOME MADE ICE CREAM
10200 Colvin Run Road, Great Falls, VA;
no phone available.
C C C G G G

You Can Still Go Home Again to Thelma's

The old country store is settling into its seventieth year and on every visit it looks even smaller, dustier, and much older. The brown asphalt siding is fading and chipping away like a receding hairline. You just can't get that kind of siding anymore. Thank goodness. My late boss Frank Forrester, former NBC weatherman and spokesman for the U.S. Geological Survey, first brought me here in the 1980s and I've been stopping ever since.

The store is aging rapidly, but not Thelma Feighery. "The Ice Cream Queen of Great Falls" just twinkled past her eighty-third birthday and is still scooping it out.

Sure, the space behind the counter now includes a walker, just in case. And maybe the gas pumps were allowed to stop working in 1990, but not Queen Thelma. For about fifty years she has been making and dishing out good ice cream.

When I talked to her in early April 1998, right after the community of Great Falls threw a birthday party for her, Thelma said, "We are just coming out of the slow time for ice cream and again starting to make about one hundred gallons a week." At that pace, Thelma has had a cold personal hand in mixing up and scooping out at least 250,000 gallons of ice cream. That's a lot of practice making perfect a family secret recipe for great ice cream.

Thelma's is, of course, much more than just ice cream. It's a dark old country store with narrow aisles where people keep bumping into each other and the jars of jawbreakers and bags of potato chips. All that bumping in the dark seems to quickly turn strangers into friends. If a bright white strip mall ice cream store is a modern ride on the Metro, then Thelma's is a creaky ride on a San Francisco cable car. Take your choice.

It's a place where truck drivers, hardened by the rapid growth and traffic snarling along nearby Route 7, still make special stops at this backwater oasis to check up on a special lady. Their lunch is an ice cream float and a chance to be scolded or hugged by a borrowed grandmother with a twinkle in her eye.

Thelma patiently waits while newcomers try to read the twenty-three flavors of ice cream listed on the faded hand-lettered sign. (Hint: don't squint, just get the black raspberry.) When a flavor is finally picked, all of the nearly five feet of Thelma seems to dive out of sight into the chest freezer before emerging triumphant, like a short Statue of Liberty, holding up your ice cream cone.

Thelma guards that faded sign carefully. Her late husband, Frank, had made it over a decade ago. Paper clips hold slips of paper to block out unavailable flavors or to announce new ones. "Don't want anyone putting scotch tape on the sign, because you can't take it off without tearing. But sometimes they sneak the tape on," Thelma said, patching the sign and getting about as mad as she's going to get. Since I was the only one in the store, I accepted the blame on behalf of the rest of the world and felt about as scolded as I was going to be.

I didn't have to pout long. The next minute Thelma was cheering me up with a warm cookie that she had just baked, and I was six years old and back in my grandmother's kitchen again. That's Thelma's.

Sad Update: As I began to recheck some favorite places for this book, I found that Thelma's Home Made Ice Cream is still there—barely—but, alas, not Thelma. She died in 2001, but her family is trying hard to keep the old store going and the homemade ice cream flowing. Stop and have a cone in memory of Thelma and all those cookies our grandmothers used to make. Colvin Run Mill Park is just down the street—a great place to walk with an ice cream cone, although you might have to share it with the ducks. I hope this write-up serves as a slight tribute to a tall little lady, fondly remembered and missed.

CHARCOAL KABAB

394 Elden Street, K-Mart Shopping Center, Herndon, VA; phone: 703-435-2400.

C C G G G

Desperately Seeking Soothing

Previous laments about my love/hate relationship with the common curry burn stirred several crummybutgood scouts to offer cures #3 and #4.

It's an old familiar story that I discussed on my visit to the Mayur Kabab House in Washington. You know the story: Young kid gets hooked on curry in Kuwait oil camp. Macho peer pressure keeps his stomach smoking from overspicing. Years later, the desire is still strong, but the stomach weak. Desperately seeking soothing, I hired an expensive spice consultant to observe my curry-eating habits. Dr. Spice offered basic solutions #1 and #2:

#1: Stop drinking water with the curry. Instead of dousing the fire, water just moves it around. Faster. And to places never designed for full-strength curry.

#2: Eat more nan (bread) and rice. It is there to help smother the fire.

Solution #3 came from the previous owner of Mayur Kabab (when it was called Shiney Kabab), who offered to mild down the spices in his restaurant. No sir, I responded, don't change the spices, fix my stomach. It's more a question of we overprotected Midwestern tenderbellys learning to adapt to the big spicy world out there.

Sympathetic First Fan Hilary Ray (Herndon, VA) suggested soothing solution #4: "My English husband and his brother generally engage in foolish curry duels whenever they are reunited. Must be a guy thing. My local CBG joint, an Afghan place called Charcoal Kabab, serves a beverage with near-mystical properties for curry neutralization. It's called 'dough' . . . sort of like yogurt in its primary stages, with the consistency of milk but quite salty and with big flakes of dried mint and chopped cucumber. It sounds and looks pretty vile, but it is completely delicious and has amazing palate-cleansing capacity."

We agree completely on the "sounds vile" part. I'm still waiting for "completely delicious" to kick in.

But let's play fair. I recruited two companions who had sworn absolute vows of no curry ever. Told them there was some dough in it for them if they would try the curry with me at Charcoal Kabab.

The specials of the day, kofta (meatball curry) and lentil-chickpea curry, came with a choice of rice or fresh tandori bread, and a hint of salad and a yogurt side dish. As I ordered the suggested curry-dousing dough drink, the counterman and a young, dark-haired woman at table number six gave me funny looks.

"Excuse me," she said. "I'm surprised because doo-gheh (she had to spell out the throat-clearing pronunciation for me) is such an acquired taste." A taste, it turns out, that she acquired as a child in Iran.

And thus I added a dough/dugh/doo-gheh expert to the vast Crummy But Good scouting staff. Sounia warned me, "Restaurants that make the drink in-house have good dugh days and not so good ones." Like I could tell. When Sounia is not trying to teach me how to write doo-gheh in Farsi-out script—it looks a lot like "Ee>," if you turn all the right angles into soft curves and dot the "E"—she still finds time to be president and CEO of a computer company.

Which is one of the nice things about CBG places like the Charcoal Kabab. An ease, even an expectation, that strangers, be they digital or be they not, will talk to each other. So what if you have to bus your own tables and pick up your own orders. So what if the atmosphere is about zero, except for a post office rouge's gallery of all the Afghan kings since about 350 B.C. So what if the glare off bare tables and walls is cold. The warmth is in the curry and chitchat and the hum of multilingual tongues. The warmth is in the long line of Middle Eastern doo-gheh experts waiting to order and willing to talk to Midwestern curry virgins. In the macho Englishmen bravely turning a burnt, stiff upper lip to the curry. And in watching my curry-fearing companions licking their plates clean while cautiously sipping their doo-gheh teaspoon by teaspoon, like castor oil.

Loudoun and Prince William Counties

BLUE RIDGE SEAFOOD

**15704 Lee Highway, Route 29, just north of Route 15
intersection, Gainesville, VA; phone: 703-754-9852.
C C C G G G**

Despite Shorts Coming, Fish Expert Approves

"I don't like waitresses who wear shorts." This is obviously not
me speaking. Rather, it is my handpicked fish expert talking as
our waitress left the table. I did not agree, but sometimes I know
enough to keep my mouth shut.

I had carefully picked as my fish expert a person who had
probably eaten fish at least once a week for 4,200 weeks, or
all eighty-plus years of her life. Someone whose church cele-
brated, by actual count, nearly two hundred days of Lent each

year. Not the easy Easter Lents I had known—"Okay, okay, I'll give up broccoli for forty days"—but two hundred tough days of meatless, bean soup, cabbage, and fish Lents. Because we so badly needed her expertise on the Crummy But Good Team, I married her daughter.

And now you know why I wisely kept my mouth shut when my Other Mother, Baba the fish expert, frowned on shorts.

Blue Ridge Seafood has received at least a half dozen nominations from readers. Rebecca Phipps (Shepherdstown, WV) said, "I've never been there, but that swimming-pool-blue roof always makes me smile. It looks like a place you should try."

Diane Noserale supplied a romantic footnote: "On their first date, friends of mine went to the Blue Ridge. Everything was going well until he realized he forgot his wallet, which was a bummer, since he had asked her out. She ended up paying. That was more than twelve years ago. They have two kids and will celebrate their tenth anniversary this fall."

All together now, everybody say "Ahhhhhhh."

Helen Blackwell (Arlington, VA) said, "As transplants from South Louisiana, my husband and I thought the name was so funny we stopped there back in 1975, and have been fans ever since. It fits your criteria: looks dumpy and seedy from the outside and has marvelous crab cakes and other seafood."

And good chicken too, according to my seafood-avoiding-after-too-many-Lents constant companion, who usually orders the chicken breast fingers basket (with coleslaw, French fries, and hush puppies). Meanwhile, Baba the fish expert pronounced the grilled swordfish "very good." Within recent memory, she ranked it second only to the Alaska salmon caught by a grandson and grilled by him the night before, which is pretty stiff competition. And yes, the crab cakes deserve consideration in the next Crab Cake War. On our last visit, I had the Blue Ridge Combination (sautéed crabcake, fried haddock, shrimp, scallops, clam strips, and hush puppies with a choice of potatoes or rice and salad or coleslaw). The price (around $26.00) seems high on the usual CBG scale, but it's a good value and enough food for two meals. I'm told that everything but the clam strips came in fresh.

The dining area is divided into an outer sanctum, an inner sanctum, and a smaller claustro-sanctum. Be careful not to fall into the large trashcan on your right as you enter the main room. On our first visit, we arrived early on a Lenten Friday, before the fish smells had overcome the bathroom disinfectant smells in the inner sanctum. The outside dining patio looked pleasant with both sun and shade sections.

The Stringer family has been running Blue Ridge Seafood since 1979. "Mom and Dad are retired now," said daughter Donna Stringer Donovan, "but we still use Mom's recipes." Good idea.

As we left the restaurant, Baba the fish expert said, "Wasn't our waitress nice?" How quickly her too-short shorts were forgiven. I may be just another shortsighted male who doesn't always agree with his mother-in-law, but I'm sometimes smart enough to know when to quietly nod my head in agreement and not say a word.

FRAN'S PLACE
Business Route 7 at the blinking light in downtown Purcellville, VA; phone: 540-338-3200.
C C C G G

Fran's Place: Just a State of Mind

Fran became a legend in western Loudoun County. An elegant, silver-haired, hardworking, friendly waitress you'd be proud to

call "Mom," even as she hollers at you for not eating the slice of tomato that always comes with breakfast. Her phenomenal memory was her trademark. She never wrote anything down, no matter how big the party. As often as we tried—once with eight people including four scrambling kids—we could never trip her up, even by changing orders and seats.

Western Loudoun applauded when son Arti Grey named his new restaurant "Fran's Place." Fran is gone now, but far from forgotten. Her picture presides over the big front table where the regular crowd sits. (For heaven's sake, don't try to sit there at lunchtime!)

First Fan Steve Scafidi (Summit Point, WV) said that Fran's Place is still a place "where a waitress can somewhat affectionately smack you in the head with a newspaper one minute and serve you delicious southern fried food the next, inexpensively!"

We have been going there for years and the place is especially busy on Saturday mornings, when old-timers in coveralls mix with the Hunt Country crowd in muddy riding boots and eager bikers in bright spandex, moist and fresh off the western end of the W&OD trail, two blocks away.

Sometimes when things get really busy, you have to get up and get your own coffee, and the custom is to offer to pour for the people in the next booth. For breakfast, I usually order the ham and cheese omelet (with toast, fried potatoes, and tomato slices). For lunch, First Fan Steve swears by the cheeseburgers and the homemade French fries. He also recommends the large Greek salad for those vegetarian moments. I have enjoyed both the hot pork sandwich (with potatoes and another vegetable) and the grilled bluefish (with homemade French fries and coleslaw or salad).

"There is nothing crummy about Fran's," said our First Fan. "It's a state of mind." Right. It's a state where you don't mind ripped cushions and mud from farm boots. Yesterday's farm boot mud. At least one *Washington Post* editor has a favorite ripped cushion that she claims fits her bottom perfectly. Just be sure to eat all your breakfast tomato. And while you're up, pour me a cup too.

PLANET WAYSIDE

Business Route 7 on the west end of Hamilton, VA,
about seven miles west of Leesburg, VA;
phone: 540-338-4315.
C C C C G G G G

[Yes, we have already reviewed Planet Wayside in the top ten section. We just couldn't resist adding owner Tim O'Neil's account of his encounter with the Secretary of State and the Secret Service. Amazing who you can meet in a Crummy But Good restaurant.]

Secretary of State Does Crummy:
Please Don't Shoot, It's Not My Purse!
By Tim O'Neil

It is just another typical night at Planet Wayside, beautiful weather, packed house, and poor service for everyone. So busy that the staff starts laughing hysterically every time the phone rang. It could be a carryout order! They might want it within their own lifetime!

Then this guy with a squiggly wire in his ear comes in and asks if there is any room for another party. I tell him there is one table left outside. He nods and as he leaves begins talking into his wrist. I'm clueless, of course, and as he exits, I yell at him, "Please don't explode on me!"

Within minutes, the patio, restaurant, and neighborhood are besieged by Secret Service men. Two point men walk in with the wrist talker, others lurk behind the patio, in the woods, by the outside bathroom, at the door to the kitchen, in the parking lot, and in the yards of the neighbors. Ten Secret Service men secretly infiltrating my restaurant, which can only hold about thirty people inside. I'm beginning to wonder if all those jokes I'd made about the little town of Hamilton getting nuclear power are coming back to haunt me. Then Madeline Albright and her guest walk in.

Fortunately for me, I recognize her and don't think it is Martha Stewart in her Secretary of State costume.

Meanwhile, back in the kitchen, life is still going on and orders are piling up, so I only get a few minutes to chat with her. The flattering thing is, she had eaten at Planet Wayside about eight years ago and returned for some barbecue in the country.

Two of the Secret Service guys order sandwiches for themselves and then go out to the patio. I yell out to them, "Hey, you guys want to be waiters?" No response. So I tell them to pick up their food at the service window. They do. A couple of more patio orders are ready, and I ask them if they would mind delivering them. They look at me as if they'd rather be nibbled by ducks.

Madame Secretary is very gracious when she leaves. I have to admit that I feel a little relieved when all ten of the Secret Service men are gone. There's something about a bunch of armed, unsmiling men just hanging out that's a little unnerving. But they were as professional as could be and obviously doing a very important job.

When I go to bus the table, I find the Secretary's purse beneath her napkin. I grab the purse and run out to the street just as the official convoy is hitting Mach 1. I yell out at the top of my lungs, "Stop! Stop!" The vehicles simultaneously start coming to a screeching halt—this is something I had seen only in the movies. One of the guys jumps out of the vehicle while it's still moving away and starts running toward me. I yell, "I've got her purse!" while praying he is not going to shoot me.

The man takes the purse from me. I swear I finally get half a smile from him. Here I am, wearing an apron over my shorts like a dress, running down the street, chasing the Secret Service, and waving a purse. The headline could have been: "Cross-Dresser Shot Stealing Secretary of State's Purse." Sometimes you just get lucky and don't get your fifteen minutes of fame.

WESTERN VIRGINIA AND WEST VIRGINIA

WARRENTON PLAZA RESTAURANT

**aka Warrenton Lanes, 272 Broadview Avenue, the old Routes 15–29–211 bypass; phone: 540-347-2300.
C C G G**

Wagner Rolling on Ice

The sound of rolling thunder followed by. . . wait for it . . . the satisfying explosions of many bowling balls taking out many pins. Good taking out evil. Or is it evil balls taking out good

pins? Either way, the sound of bowling has a primitive satis-faction to it, a roll of drums, the clash of symbols.

But can you dine to it? Out of about two hundred CBG restaurant scouting reports submitted by readers, so far only Nancy Hughes (Culpeper, VA) has nominated a bowling alley restaurant.

So when the February ice storm cometh and the electric power wenteth, we headeth southeth, which broughteth us to Warrenton on a cold Saturday morning. On a day when Washington was not so power full, the Warrenton Plaza Restaurant and Lanes had power to spare . . . and strike.

First Fan Nancy warned us that the restaurant is often crowd-ed at lunchtime during the week, "because so many locals make it a regular place to eat." But what about breakfast on an icy Saturday morning?

We were in luck. "We don't serve breakfast, except today," our Saturday host said. "On Saturday mornings we have break-fast sandwiches because of all the kids bowling early." Good fried egg sandwiches with bacon or ham and decent coffee. All served by a waitress in a bowling shirt who waited just to bowl.

Ahhh. A Wagnerian breakfast, served up by a good woman warrior to the thunder and crash of bowling balls and falling pins. Good loudly knocking down evil, except for the fearful 7–10 split, the two-fang grin of the devil himself. Be assured that on this Saturday morning, while Washington shivered under its nonelectric blanket, in Warrenton the grinning devil was under constant attack by well-behaved kids from a smaller town. To echo the words of the ancient cartographer filling in a map's dreaded blank space of unexplored territory, "Here there be Ozzie and Harriet."

For a follow-up visit, I picked a quiet Wednesday noon, before the bowling began. Two immediate good signs: the place was completely full and the diners included four sheriffs, which is like an automatic four stars in the CBG guidebook. Unfortunately, it was hamburger steak day (Special #1, with macaroni and cheese, mixed vegetables, and drink). It can be hard to get hamburger steak past the kissing-your-cousin level on the culinary excitement scale. My companion tried Special #3 (eight-ounce cheeseburger, French fries, and drink). "At last, a real hamburger," he said. But I don't think he gets out very much. I'd recommend calling ahead to see how special the special really is and if there is a lane open.

I'd also recommend picking a non-icy day when you can wander around on the drive down to Warrenton. Sure, you can go straight down Route 29 from the Beltway. More scenic is taking I–66 west and then Route 17 south. Best of all is taking Route 50 west, and once past Middleburg, taking any paved road south. Yes, you will probably get lost on your way to a Wagnerian meal, but it's great horse country to get lost in, sort of a Valkyrie me back to old Virginny route.

Dee Dee's Family Restaurant

502 North Main Street, Culpeper, VA;
phone: 540-825-4700.
C C G G G

Dee Place in Culpeper

So I'm easily confused. Dee Dee's Restaurant in Culpeper, VA, was nominated for the crummybutgood list, and I hurried south to try to get there in time for breakfast.

I took the first Culpeper exit off Route 29, and just before I reached town, I suddenly saw the sign for the Double D Restaurant out of the corner of my left eye. One U-turn later, I was rushing in the door to beat the 11:15 breakfast curfew.

The waitress seemed startled to see me walk past the bar and sit down at the cleanest table in the darkened restaurant. "We're not open," she said.

"But I called and someone said I could still get breakfast," I protested.

"We don't serve breakfast," she said. Then somewhat wistfully, "You must mean Dee Dee's Restaurant. I'd love to join you there for pancakes."

Which she should have, because at her suggestion I had three buttermilk pancakes with a side of simmered apples, and they were great. The simmered apples put Dee Dee's on my constant companion's must-stop breakfast list. You can also count on their good daily specials and barbecue pit. My companion enjoyed the ma-and-pa interior, the clean white walls and wallpaper that are backdrop to the grandma's attic collection, from scrubboard to small mirrors wearing large horse collars.

All of which begs the primary question, Is it crummy, or is it not? As First Fan Mary Gallagher (Arlington, VA) said, "I can't really say it's crummy, but it hasn't been updated for some time." Which describes many of us.

PINE GROVE RESTAURANT

Pine Grove, VA, on Route 679, a right-hand turn just after Route 7 passes through the mountain gap—Snicker's Gap—and starts down to the Shenandoah River, about eight miles west of Purcellville, VA; Phone: 540-554-8181.

C C G G

Please Pass the Pepper and the Past

If you're lucky on a Saturday morning, the place will be jammed. You'll be forced to sit at the big table with some old-timers and hear about yesterday on this Blue Ridge mountain. Back when your tablemate worked at a CCC camp during the Depression and logged timber with a team of horses. When the trains ran regular along the W&OD tracks as far as nearby Bluemont, bringing out city folks trying to escape the summer heat and taking back milk and hidden bottles of moonshine.

While you listen, gray-haired ladies visit, skipping slowly from table to table, like silver butterflies returning to remembered flower gardens.

Now the W&OD is a biking and hiking trail that brings slick pastel-shaded suburban bikers all the way out to Purcellville. The last seven-mile link of the W&OD to Bluemont is not yet complete, but you can feel it closing. A mile away, on the other side of Snicker's Gap, the two dozen homes of Pine Grove sit on old Route 7, a forgotten loop off the modern highway. As I sit listening at the table, I try not to be part of what is shrinking this last mountain holdout of the rural past.

Oh yes, the food. Breakfast is obviously a favorite time. I usually settle in with a ham and egg omelet, wheat toast, and endless coffee. My constant companion likes the blueberry hot cakes.

Lunch never seems quite as good. It's harder to get seated at the big table. The waitress always adds a nice dash of verbal sparring spice and the dozen side dishes—applesauce to pickled beets—add variety. I especially like the sweet coleslaw. My admittedly frozen liver and onions dinner was tasty. My companion swears by the BLT.

Unless you're a hiker coming off the Appalachian Trail, about a mile away, or a construction worker on a short break, food seems secondary here. We climbed this last mountain of Loudoun County and passed through Snicker's Gap in hopes of remembering and tasting the recent past.

JANE'S LUNCH

**3 East Main Street,
Berryville, VA;
phone: 540-955-3480.
C C G G G**

BON MATIN
BAKERY-CAFÉ

**1 East Main Street,
Berryville, VA;
phone: 540-955-1554.
C G G G G**

Grandma's American Cooking Meets French Pastry

Such a deal. Here they are, side by side, down-home cooking just like Grandma's and pastry with a proud French twist and pout. There are some who mix the two, picking up an éclair from Bon Matin to have with their coffee at Jane's while they wait for Jane's daughter to fix breakfast.

Jane's daughter—AKA Mitzie Myers—is the third generation to run Jane's restaurant, which has been a gather-and-gossip center at one location or another in Berryville since 1943. "A lot of our customers have been coming here for years, and they expect certain dishes fixed just the way Grandmother did. So we do," said Mitzie. "The coleslaw has her cooked egg dressing, which my own kids don't like. The meatloaf special every other Monday is fixed with vegetable soup, and the roast beef gravy is made with real drippings, not those little cubes of boullion. And of course we make our own soups and chili and cut all the meat ourselves." Of course.

Out of pure selfishness, I have decided not to mention the usual Tuesday special of chicken and dumplings or the roast chicken with homemade stuffing that often appears on Wednesdays. Breakfast on Saturday mornings—"no fast food on Saturday mornings"—can be busy and slow, but it's a nice busy and slow that lets you chat or read the paper. Some will play the Ms. Packman machine to help get back to a 1980s mood or to burn off energy from a plattercake, eggs, and scrapple breakfast. But most of us just sit and drink an extra cup of coffee to salute Grandma's cooking.

Or you can go next door to Bon Matin for a bit of down-home elegance, Berryville style. A place where owner and chief pastry chef Jean-Francois Martin speaks with a French accent that makes me nervous and his fruit tarts are just too pretty to be eaten by a clod like me. My wife and daughter love the place and say my towering delusions of French inadequacy are all in my head. Probably so. Meanwhile, I have never met a Bon Matin salad or fresh quiche du jour that I didn't like, even though we real flannel-shirted men don't eat quiche or say "du jour" out loud. Somehow my family can't seem to celebrate a big holiday without a chocolate raspberry cake from Bon Matin. If I don't mend my ways, they may start celebrating without me.

John's Family Restaurant

Route 340, north of Berryville, VA, in Rippon, WV;
phone: 304-725-4348.

C C G G G

Grouchy Wet Bottom Seeks Prayer

When searching out perfect fall apples and leaves (male CBGers tend not to say "fall foliage"), I usually head west out of Virginia on Route 7, past Leesburg, through Snicker's Gap and on across the Shenandoah River. Then I like to just wander aimlessly on any of the mountain or valley roads.

Endless riding of the roads is not, however, for everyone. On this trip my constant companion suggested that we "do a little shopping too." On my free-time pursuits calendar, shopping comes somewhere after dental work. Reluctantly, peevishly, I headed north with a pout on Route 340 toward Shepherdstown, a favorite "little shopping" town.

Along the way on Route 340, about five miles north of Berryville, VA, is John's Family Restaurant. A good CBG if you are flying grouchy or on a wing without a prayer. The knick-knacks at John's can help distract the grouchies, and the menu and placemats provide a variety of short prayers, just in case you're suffering from that sort of deficiency.

John's country flavor includes quilts on the ceiling, an antique wooden portable potty displayed on the eat-in porch, and a cowbell that rings when an order is ready. There are, however, some strict hand-written rules posted: "Employees: You do not sit with the customers."

Still in a grouchy mood, I tried not to show interest in the nineteen different vegetables and side dishes listed on the menu. My companion, the shopper, enjoyed sweet potato fries and apple sticks with her egg-and-sausage sandwich. I ordered liver and onions, a defiant gesture designed to get a rise out of my liver-despising tablemate. "West Virginia is for livers," I muttered. She ignored me and my liver.

The meat was tender and generously smothered in onions. Because of all the onions, plus the two vegetables (I chose sweet potatoes and baked beans) I loudly demanded full credit for a vegetarian credit. Again I was ignored.

Trying to remain grouchy, I started arguing with the home-made peach cobbler. Shoofly pie should have a wet bottom, but a cobbler should not. A proper cobbler is a clash of two worlds: one dry and crumbly and one fruity and syrupy. The two worlds should be cobbled together, yet remain distinctly different.

The peach cobbler didn't respond, but my companion did. She sent me to my room. She told me to go outside and cool off so that she could finish eating the rest of my perfectly good dessert in peace.

LAUDER'S RESTAURANT

583 West Strasburg Road—Route 55—about one mile from the Riverton exit on Route 340 and about three miles south from the Route 340 exit of I-66, Front Royal, VA; phone: 540-635-5121.
C C C G G G

Coleslaw Heaven

The leaves were just beginning to change, the distressed trees near the road cuts a bright red and yellow, the rest still a dusty, droughty green. Daydreaming dusty colors and thoughts, I drove right past Lauder's, which is easy to do. The small red brick building crouches downhill behind a gravel parking lot and screams nondescript.

Equally surprising is the coleslaw connection. I've been enjoying Mrs. Lauder's coleslaw ever since the deli manager at the local supermarket recommended it several years ago. Surely this tiny restaurant in the middle of Blue Ridge nowhere wasn't delivering fresh coleslaw to stores forty miles away?

"Yep. That's us," said Mrs. Lauder's son Carson. "Deliver it myself. We process about 350 pounds of cabbage daily, five or six days a week. Did about a thousand pounds just for the last Fourth of July." He proudly showed me the small kitchen and the home-sized appliances that chop up all that coleslaw and mix all that dressing.

You need a lot of cholesterol to balance the fresh, sharp-tasting coleslaw. First Fan Walter Campbell (Arlington, VA) recommended "the Saumberger platter" (large patty of country sausage covered by a slice of cheese and a 100 percent beef hamburger patty, topped with steam-fried onions, and served on a Kaiser roll with French fries and coleslaw and coffee, iced tea, or soft drink with free refills). I added a dozen apple sticks (diced apples, batter dipped and deep fried), which turned out to be a great snack, hot or cold.

The tired-but-friendly restaurant is probably little changed since Mrs. Lauder opened for breakfast back in July 1966. No yucky gray duct tape here; seats are mended with classy clear plastic tape.

Our CBG Scout Campbell suggested combining a Lauder visit with a stop at the Linden Vineyards (540-364-1997). "Either stay on 55 (east) or take I-66 to the Linden exit (exit 13) and follow 55 east to Route 638. They have a beautiful view from the outdoor deck and sell French bread and cheese to go with the wine."

A loaf of bread, a bottle of wine, and a quart of Mrs. Lauder's coleslaw. And thou of course. Sounds like a perfect crummybutgood day.

INSPIRATIONS BAKERY, CAFE AND BED AND BREAKFAST

174 North Washington Street, Berkeley Springs, WV; phone: 304-258-2292.

C G G G G

For Inspirations, Try a Bath

Have to admit to some prejudice here. We have a weekend cabin about two ridges west of Berkeley Springs, on the old mountain road between Great Cacapon and Paw Paw. I also write a column, The Weekender, for the local weekly paper, the *Morgan Messenger*. So I'm partial to Berkeley Springs, but I might as well stick to the prejudices that I know best.

The core old town is officially Bath, while the post office for the larger region is officially Berkeley Springs. The place has always had something of a split personality. For several hundred years, the warm springs and their alleged curative bathing powers have drawn both tourists and the people who make their living off tourists. At the same time, there is a strong-minded local population that calls Berkeley Springs home and over the years has done fine, thank you very much, as railroad builders, sand miners, tomato canners, and textile sewers, or whatever living the work of the times will provide.

In recent years the resident artist community has grown and become more visible, to the point that Berkeley Springs has been listed among the top one hundred artist communities and recently made *USA Today's* Top Ten list.

Me? I just like to sit back and watch the parade. Best place is sitting on the porch of the Inspirations Bakery and Cafe on a Sunday morning. There is still a lot of semitruck traffic on Route 522 that roars through town, mixed with antique cars heading for a car show somewhere and the endless cruising of pickup trucks. Yet the pace remains small town slow. Locals drift up and down the street, to the laundromat or 7–11 that sits across the way, or maybe to the nearby secondhand store or funeral parlor. The locals sometimes call the tourists "shorts," and it's easy to see why in the overexposed white legs of early summer that walk hesitantly along the sidewalk, pausing at menus and historic plaques. Lots of history here. George Washington not only slept here, he bathed, surveyed, and marched here. Place even has a castle with a ghost and a romantic past. Mixed in the parade with the locals and the shorts are the wandering weavers, writers, painters, and iron smiths, often on their way to the nearby ugly Ice House that has been converted into an artist studio, gallery, and workshop.

Meanwhile we sit back on the Inspirations porch where we couldn't ask for a better view or a better breakfast or lunch. The small menu will surprise you with its variety. For breakfast, I usually have the morning wrap (scrambled eggs, bacon, scallions, and cheddar cheese rolled in a flour tortilla) or the smoked salmon platter (with cream cheese, red onions, and a bagel). The coffee is extra good and many of the mugs have been snuck in by regulars like us just to make the place feel more like home. At lunchtime, my wife, my constant companion, hopes that the former regular treat on the menu—the Black Forest sandwich (a hot medium-rare roast beef sandwich with lots of horseradish and coleslaw)—will again be featured. If not, you can't go wrong with the specials. Inspirations is also a B&B with three rooms with private baths.

And I haven't even mentioned the pastries yet. Just be sure to leave some brownies for me.

WARM SPRINGS RESTAURANT

On U.S. Route 522, south end of Berkeley Springs, WV; phone: 304-258-2188.

C C G G G

Revenge of the Grouchy Sisters

Thirty years ago, the former owners, two grandmotherly sisters, dared to holler at our darling perfect children. The Warm Springs Restaurant immediately became known in our family as the "Grouchy Sisters Restaurant." We were indignant as only green parents can be. What's wrong with our healthy red-blooded five-year-old boy trying to get all the counter stools swiveling at the same time? Why should our three-year-old daughter be denied the pleasure of playing with all the knickknacks the restaurant has displayed to sell?

In keen hindsight developed over the past twenty years of searching for the perfect crummybutgood restaurant, we now know the sisters were absolutely right. Our little darlings deserved the hollering and their parents should have served time in the dumpster. Annoyance by others is not a mandatory part of dining out, even in CBG restaurants.

We still go back. The sisters are gone now and we never had a chance to thank them or apologize. But the Warm Springs Restaurant remains a good stop, especially on the autumn leaf and apple butter tour. A place for basic country food, well prepared, where the potatoes are real and served by a waitress with a genuine nonplastic country smile. The counter stools are still there if you'd like to take them for a spin, and there are plenty of knickknacks left to look over. Meals are reasonably priced, unless your companion buys one of the quilts.

The daily specials are usually good. I recently enjoyed the pork and sauerkraut (with mashed potatoes, gravy, a vegetable, and rolls). My constant companion, mother of the brats, likes the Berkeley Club (with ham, lettuce, tomato, American cheese, bacon, mayo, and chips).

(Question: Why would anyone advertise that they use a cheese that bland? I'm not un-American, but why not just say "cheese" and hope nobody notices that it is boring cheese? Or is the reassurance of boring cheese one of those CBG traditions that I don't understand?)

One welcomed addition is Ruth, who gets star billing on the menu for her fresh pies and homemade carrot cake. My pumpkin pie tasted like it came from a fresh pumpkin and not a can.

Entertainment with our dessert was provided by one of the many Berkeley Springs town characters, who shared with us a long description of all his troubles forty years ago in high school. He was obviously part of the revenge of the Grouchy Sisters for the long-ago misbehavior of our bratty kids. At least when we got our just desserts they weren't Ruth-less.

MOBY DICK HOUSE OF KABOB

1070 31st Street NW, Georgetown, Washington, DC;
phone: 202-333-4400.
C C C C G G G

Lots of Elbows, Not Much Room

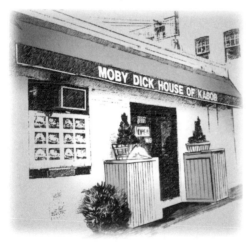

Sometimes you just feel like going to a restaurant that's slightly smaller than a broom closet. But that's you, not me.

In that spirit of extreme togetherness, First Fan Eric Wenocur (Silver Spring, MD) enthusiastically nominated Moby Dick House of Kabob in Georgetown: "The chicken kabob is the best thing that has happened to chicken in my lifetime. The locale just happens to be a dire hole-in-the-wall."

When it comes to chicken, Fan Eric obviously has led a very sheltered life. But he sure knows his holes-in-the-wall. One of my dining companions ordered the chicken kabob sandwich-kabob-e joojeh, skinless fat-free chunks of chicken marinated in special house seasoning, on pita bread—and we all agreed it was good. Better than my lamb or the ground sirloin of companion B. When I go back, I want to try some of the yogurt side dishes that looked so good as the cook passed them under my nose and hollered, "Number 17!"

My nose was seated tight up against the menu wall, next to the takeout counter. Moby Dick is not your whale-size hole-in-the-wall. I'd guess it would seat twelve in reasonable uncomfortableness. At one point, I counted twenty-two heads trying to be inside the restaurant, either ordering, waiting to order, picking up, or actually eating. Not a place or time to ask a lot of questions. So I still don't know how a Persian restaurant got the name "Moby Dick." Nor do I know the name of the strange clay oven that I could see behind the counter where pita bread was constantly baking. In honor of Herman Melville, let's call the oven "Ishmael."

Ishmael the oven has baked endless loaves of the fresh bread that is definitely one of the special treats at Moby Dick's. Half the customers ordered food by Persian names in non-English sentences, which both encouraged and intimidated us obvious tourists who sheepishly ordered by the Arabic numbers. If you go on a busy Friday afternoon, best take a plan B with you, an idea of where to go to eat if all the inside spaces are taken. Because I'm sure not going to give up my seat, now that I know how to throw an elbow without spilling my rice.

* * *

Footnote: Crummy But Good scouts try so hard to make me smarter. Which is about as easy as making broccoli smell good. My initial review of Moby Dick produced a particular outpouring.

"Why is it called Moby Dick?" I asked. Several readers responded like CBG Fan Steve Olson, "Moby Dick was the name of a very popular restaurant in Tehran before the revolution, hence the name." But CBG Fan Jim Zurer said the Bethesda manager of Moby Dick claimed he happened to have been reading the book "when the restaurant was being planned and really liked the book and hence the name."

I also suggested that the name of the oven that baked the sheet bread was either "tandoor" or "Ishmael." Some of you agreed with "tandoor," but others, like Sassan Ghari, said the Persian name is "tanoor" and the Indian oven is a "tandoor." In a follow-up visit, we found the chicken and tenderloin combination outstanding, both meats juicy, tender, and well seasoned. Manager Hossein Eghtedari confirmed that the oven was indeed a tanoor and then bravely went on to explain the four typical varieties of nan (bread) that could be served in a Persian restaurant. The thin, holey bread that they bake and serve fresh and that is called pita on the menu and by most of us is really "taftoon."

Thank you scouts for all the help. Now lets get back to the bigger mission of making broccoli smell good.

BISTRO ITALIANO
320 D Street NE, Washington, DC;
phone: 202-546-4522.
C C G G G

Philodendron on the Rack

Sometime during the training at the Crummy But Good Culinary Institute, a course is taught in cruelty to plants. Future

waitresses, cooks, and restaurant owners learn that plants are just dying to grow in any dark nook or cranny. And die they do. But slowly.

Slowly but invisible to staff and longtime patrons, the struggling plants—two-leafed African violets, brown spider plants, tired dusty cacti, and geraniums without hope—become part of the woodwork, unnoticed and unwatered, except when there is nothing else to do. Best to keep the plants dry so the Boss doesn't think you don't have enough to do. The most common CBG plant torture is philodendron on the rack. Long, almost leafless vines of philodendron are strung on strings across the walls and ceilings of CBG restaurants everywhere.

Which was just about the crummiest thing we could find inside Bistro Italiano. We almost retreated in uncrummy defeat from the bright white and purple walls and matching cloth napkins and tablecloths and the real flowers on half the tables. Fortunately the tablecloths were kept under practical plastic wrap, half the tables had plastic flowers, and enough deliverymen wandered through the small eleven-table dining area to make us feel at home. And always, on the ceiling above it all, were the traditional strings of painfully pale philodendron.

We didn't retreat. The kitchen smelled too good and the

place felt too right, too neighborly, to leave. One word of warning: If your companion, like mine, is a hibernating bear just shaking off a Blue Ridge winter, don't let him sit near the seminaked Greek woman in the single-breasted toga. Despite being mere plaster and less than three feet high, her spell caused notable lapses in his culinary conversation.

"From the outside you could mistake Bistro Italiano for one of the many dry-cleaning establishments on Capitol Hill," cautioned First Fan Neil Scott (Washington, DC).

This First Fan is no fly-by-nighter when it comes to restaurant stakeouts. "At least four restaurants have failed here over the past twenty years," Scott noted in his detailed report. "In the past it was a Greek carryout run by Koreans; a fast food place run by a guy with hairy biceps; and a Peruvian chicken carryout run by, of all people, Peruvians. Now it is an Italian restaurant run by two Caucasians, a Korean, and an Iranian cook who looks French." (The Iranian has since been replaced by a new partner from El Salvador and another who is Irish-American but grew up on Italian cooking.)

"How do I know it's good?" First Fan Neil said. "I saw a Domino Pizza delivery guy walking out with one of their pizzas."

At Scott's suggestion, we focused on the subs and sandwiches, particularly the chicken souvlaki on fresh-baked pita bread (served with French fries, lettuce, tomato, onion, feta cheese, and yogurt dressing). The bread was extra tasty and we were surprised to discover it was made from the pizza dough. Almost as good was the veal parmigiana sub. We split an order of spaghetti and tried to ignore the French fries, especially when we discovered the nice subtle bite in the spaghetti sauce. As a reward for ignoring most of the French fries, we overindulged in sinful fresh-made cannoli. A classic case of being fries wise and cannoli foolish.

MAYUR KABAB HOUSE

1108 K Street NW, Washington, DC; free marked parking in the alley for the brave and the lucky; phone: 202-637-9770.

C C C C G G

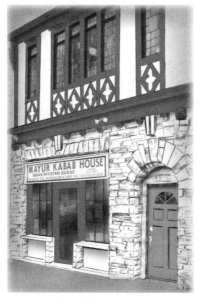

Lips That Touch Curry . . .

Everyone remembers the first time. Not just your first kiss of curry, but the first full-body experience. A burning fire that no water can quench. The sweat, the tears, the brave smile on the morning after.

My first curry came in Kuwait. As the youngest greenhorn in a tough oil camp, it was important that I smile and make yummy noises all through the hot curried goat supper we had every Thursday. On Fridays, our macho therapy group would discuss in great detail just where the curry was at that particular moment. Eating and discussing curry with a sweaty smile became yet another test of manhood.

The new camp cook was subjected to the same greenhorn harassment. Pauli arrived from Baluchistan speaking no English, which egged on his tormentors. In revenge, the curry got stronger week after week.

Finally Pauli struck the coup de curry. On the third Thursday, he piled an unusually dark curried meat onto the plate of our Chief Tormentor.

CT, a constipated Texas rattlesnake, looked at the dark meat and gave Pauli a deep warning grunt and a hard questioning look as he shook the plate at the cook.

"Goat," said Pauli, proud of his growing English vocabulary.

"One hump or two?" asked CT slowly.

"Maybe goat," said Pauli, with a mean little smile. A smile that said I am the cook and old camel meat could be the least of your future dining problems.

CT wisely stopped harassing the cook. Besides, after one bite of Pauli's full-body curry, who could tell what kind of meat it was anyway?

Moral: Never curry disfavor with the cook.

Ever since Kuwait, I haven't been a big fan of hot spices. Maybe I got burned out. Trying to recover the lost macho of my youth, I took my hot spice specialist to the Kabab House for advice. First Fan Lori Sampson (Garrett Park, MD) assured me that it was "a hole-in-the-wall with great kababs." After watching me eat, my spice specialist said, "Stop drinking so much water. The rice and the nan (fresh flat bread) are there to soak up the fire. The water just moves the fire around." Now he tells me.

On that first visit, we arrived early for lunch (11:00) and were surrounded by cabbies rushing to get back on the road to catch the rich lunch crowd. Here is a good place to finish all those conversations that began with "Where to?"

We tried the lunch buffet, and our choices included cauliflower with potatoes, lamb and potato curry, and chicken curry. Tasty, spicy, and filling, especially if you are into the brown food groups. Like a country stew, everything was slowly simmering brownward, even the potatoes and the peas.

My second visit was a late lunch (1:30) and the crowd was

mostly shirt-and-tie men and well-heeled women arguing office politics. I ordered a special that provided enough kabab, rice, vegetable, nan, and salad to feed two. A nice combination of lamb kabab, chicken kabab, and chicken tikka, all marinated with house spices and slow cooked over charcoal.

I especially enjoyed the first two bites—then my lips turned numb and I couldn't tell if my chicken had been kababed or tikked. Not trusting my numb lips, I asked the gentleman at the next table how he would rate the kababs. "I'm the wrong one to ask," he said. "I come here about three times a week." Ah, a true numb kabab junky. I asked manager Kumar what the difference was between a "kabab" and a "kabob." He said they are the same thing, but in this story we'll stick with his kababs.

I have hopes that curry and the new mature me will get along better the second time around. At least now I know not to drink and curry.

CENTRAL MARYLAND

TASTEE DINER

8601 Cameron Street, a block off Georgia Avenue, Silver Spring, MD; phone: 301-589-8171; www.tasteediner.com.
C G G G

Will Success Spoil Old Silver Sides?

Is bigger better? Can you make a successful silk purse out of a comfortable old sow's ear? Can a favorite old CBG diner improve too much? Join me in an experiment in progress.

In July 1997, I wrote the following review of the Tastee Diner for the *Washington Post:*

I can't say "no" to a real silver-sided metal diner that proudly says I was born out of World War II and have been here 50 years. And when the waitress pulled my pat of butter out of her apron pocket, I knew I was home.

The diner is not so much crummy as just well aged, like a fine aluminum wine just reaching its peak. A favorite old grandmother with lots of wrinkles and worn spots and strands of hair out of place, whom you would follow anywhere for some of her cooking and a pat on the head.

Probably not the place you'd go to impress a first date. Unless, of course, you have found the perfect date. One who understands the beauty of crummy greatness, who shares the need to rub elbows on Formica tables, and who wants to run her fingers through the old tunes on a tabletop jukebox.

A place where my North Carolina friend could say, "Now this is real country ham." A place where the milk-shakes are so thick you can stand a knife up in the foam and the Cheeseburger Royal ($4.95 with fries and coleslaw) makes you cry over all the time you've wasted on drive-in burgers. And while we're on this high, let's just ignore the beef stew.

First Fan and local historian Jerry McCoy recommended the creamed chipped beef over biscuits as the best for breakfast (available anytime after midnight). "You can skip lunch if you have this one." But hurry. The Tastee Diner was scheduled to be moved a few blocks, and who knows how well World War II will travel?

That's what I said, and travel, it did, moving a few blocks uptown in June 2000. How well did it travel? The crummybut-good vote is still out.

We don't want to vote too quickly, because CBGers can too easily slide into a superior and antichange frame of mind. Sometimes we hanker too quickly for the good old days. Sometimes we remember imagined yesterday times as always good and past places as always better, when in fact neither was neither. We sometimes conveniently forget wars and diseases and pimples and unrest and bad coffee and thin soups that were also part of our good old days and good old places.

So let it be with the new Tastee Diner. Let's give it a chance to get comfortable again.

The new diner has more than doubled in size and now can seat over three hundred, which is stretching my concept of a diner as being a trolley car with a counter, six booths, and a cook and a waitress who yell at each other. The counter remains in what looks like the original diner, which is mostly now a reception area to the larger wings added on either side. Our old diner now has a Web site, an ATM machine, a computer to check out your e-mail, and patio dining. Our remembered crew of comfortable older waitresses who reminded you of a busy mom and carried butter in their pockets is being replaced by a younger generation of with-it waitresses who look cool in Tastee Diner T-shirts.

The place feels so new that it's hard to hang a crummy "C" on it, except for historical reasons. The menu has remained pretty much the same, except beer and wine are now available. The Cheeseburger Royal remains good and the price unchanged, but the creamed chipped beef over biscuits is less dependable and officially footnoted as "when available."

The growing numbers of sleek-seeking customers probably haven't noticed the slow demise of both the old diner and the fatty and filling creamed chipped beef. Still, it was good to see young families and singles enjoy the new old diner, eating late breakfasts together before the office lunch crowd swarmed in. Looking comfortable, like a CBG crowd should. Maybe we old-timers could be pretty happy with the new Tastee Diner if we just didn't have the old diner on our mind. Let's give it another day, and then we'll vote.

NICK'S DINER

11199 Viers Mill Road, at the corner of University Boulevard, Wheaton, MD; phone: 301-933-5459. C C C G G G

If Today Is Meatloaf, It Must Be Wednesday

Now here is the trolley car diner. Remember that little diner back home, where regular people went? Where for years the same faces sat in the same places on the right days to order their favorite daily special? And some specials tasted better than Mom's home cooking, which of course you never said out loud. And everyone who cooked and served your food was

related to the owner? A place where you could count on the same little old ladies saying with mock surprise on every visit, "I don't think I can finish this. Can you wrap it up?"

That back-home place has moved to Wheaton. Just ask ten-year-plus First Fans Frank and Henrietta Leimbach (Silver Spring, MD). "Hard to find a place that has, for such reasonable prices, a steady, every day different hot meal special," the Leimbachs wrote. They recommend Monday, also called spaghetti-with-meat-sauce day. We were running slow and didn't get there until meatloaf day, which in some regions is mistakenly called Wednesday. The meatloaf comes with mashed potatoes and long-simmered peas or green beans. My constant companion declared it a good meal and a half. The waitress said, "Breakfast anytime." So I tried the feta cheese and gyro omelet. Why? Because it was there. Interesting, but I'll stick to feta and feta in my next Greek omelet.

I asked Nick what seemed to give his meatloaf a pleasant little kick. Not pepper, not onion, not Worcestershire sauce. "Maybe the dill," he said. Maybe he wasn't telling me everything. And maybe it was just me, feeling back home and guiltily enjoying better-than-Mom's meatloaf.

Oh sure, Mom keeps a cleaner house and her driveway is

much easier to park in. So give Nick a few crummy "C"s. But I can't count on Mom to have baked lamb or Athenian chicken on Fridays. Give Nick some of Mom's extra "G"s.

HAPPY ITALIAN DELIGHT
Free State Mall, Route 450, eastern Bowie, MD; phone: 301-262-4350.
C C C G G G

"Barca, Barca," Said the Cave Dog

Being in a strip mall really helps on the crummy scale, adding at least one "C" for sterile surroundings. Still, I took to the place instantly, maybe because I appreciate a restaurant with regular customers, where the cook can greet the person in front of me with a cheery, "You'll never guess who died."

I quickly looked at the seated customers to see if I could guess which one was dead and what exactly on the menu did it. But everyone at this crowded spot—mall rats, clerks on breaks, and mothers with squirmy children—looked content with living and many bore a telltale tattoo of tomato sauce. For the moment, happy Italians all.

When I visit the Happy Italian, the sensible members of my

family expect me to bring home a vegetarian calzone (fresh dough filled with ricotta, eggplant, mushrooms, green peppers, and mozzarella). The Neanderthals among us prefer the Sicilian barca (fresh dough filled with sausage, meatballs, mushrooms, green peppers, onions, and mozzarella), but we will also take any calzone that falls our way. Both crispy-crusted meals travel and reheat well.

This is also one of those places that demonstrate a wise-balance between short-cuts and long-cuts. For torn vinyl seats, a quick dab of duct tape will do. But for the bread, nothing but slow baking daily to produce a crust that shows character and will never touch plastic. We must keep our priorities straight.

Moon Café

137 Prince George Street, a block from the City Docks, Annapolis, MD; phone: 410-280-1956.
C C G G G

Attack of the Vegans!

It happened right there on the corner of Prince George and Randall Streets, not far from the Naval Academy and the City Docks, between the astrologer's place and the barbershop with the lusty babes on the door. The Moon Cafe. Both meat and vegan, twenty hot teas and one purple goo. Worn linoleum on the floor and thick rugs on the tables.

Is it a fun but confusing place? A meeting place for locals, tourists, and Johnnies from St. John's College? A refuge for

endangered beatniks waiting for the Monday night poetry readings? Yes.

I was nagged into going by one of Them. "Despite the fact that you never went to Arianas in Severna Park, here is another recommendation," wrote First Fan Barbara Cantor (Edgewater, MD), a known Vegetarian. "The tiny hole-in-the-wall called the Moon Cafe has just been taken over by Fahima of Arianas fame. The sandwiches are big and on good breads, they have a special drink my daughter loves called Purple Goo . . . and you can savor Arianas homemade hummus."

I would never under my own free will drive eighty miles to savor hummus. If I did, how could I ever look John Wayne, Clint Eastwood, or my three brothers in their collective macho eyes? But the curry chicken was fresh and pretty darn good (with rice, vegetables, and bread). A nice light, kiss-and-run curry that holds your interest briefly and then lets you go back to the office without any lingering internal regrets. Best to ignore the accompanying mixed vegetables, the kind you keep frozen at home as an emergency fix to punish unexpected guests.

The rougher of my two companions enjoyed his Greek Gyro

(lettuce, tomato, onion, cucumber, and gyro lamb meat on pita bread and topped with a yogurt sauce). He found it tasty, but it seemed a bit dry to me.

Second Fan Kate Naughten, our Vegan-speaking guide and companion, insisted that we try the stuffed grape leaves (six grape leaves stuffed right there with rice and Middle Eastern herbs) and the Purple Goo. I'm glad we brought her and her sneaky good tastes along. The stuffed grape leaves, pita bread, and Goo were delightful high points of the meal. Maybe it was the three straws we shared in the tall glass of Goo. Maybe it was guessing its contents—"made with fresh fruit, fruit juices, ice and secret ingredients." Maybe it was our token Vegan Person being smart enough in the ways of diehard Neanderthals not to tell us we were sharing a "sugar-free, dairy-free, vitamin and mineral-packed health shake."

She even fooled me with a taste of her "hamburger." In reality a Moon Burger, which came billed as "strong enough for a carnivore but made for a vegan. All soy products, no fat and only 84 calories!" (with tortilla chips, lettuce, tomato, onion, and an optional touch of brie).

After the meal, my carnivore companion and I walked outside nervously. We stared at the lusty but fading pictures on the barbershop door, hoping they would protect us from the evil forces of Vegan, which is like betting on day-old garlic against sneaky vampires. How long have these alien Vegans walked among us and fooled us with their soy-full phony meat products? Are we all hopelessly hooked on tofu already? Did I actually say the Goo was "delightful"? Would I soon lose the ability to walk on my knuckles?

On the brighter side, I now had another excuse to call Agent Scully and report a possible X-File. Maybe this time she'll return my call. Man cannot live by soy alone.

PEE WEE'S PLACE

158 West Central Avenue, Edgewater, MD;
phone: 401-956-4072.
C C C C G G

Big Welcome at a Peewee Place

A big yes on both crummy and friendly atmosphere, but I needed a second opinion on the food. On my first visit, the spaghetti on Spaghetti Night was okay, but I arrived late and the pasta was getting tough and the clam sauce was turning cold and, well . . . clammy.

But not my fellow diners. A constant coming and going, but always a dozen people in and everyone knew and greeted everyone else, even me, an obvious stranger. One of the definite pluses in small barroom dining is that you are part of every conversation and only get left out if you want to be. No, on second thought, there is no way to be left out.

First Fan Caroline Reutter said, "I'm from South Carolina and this is where I go for good downhome cooking."

So, save yourself a trip to Carolina. Go to Pee Wee's Place instead. Caroline particularly recommended the oyster stew, and I have to agree. On my second visit I dove into a big bowl of stew with lots of oysters in creamy broth. My constant companion bravely ordered that day's special, a foot-long hot dog with chili sauce, which turned out to be enough to last her for at least two lunches.

In the daylight, we couldn't find a sign saying "Pee Wee's Place." Taking a chance, we parked and walked to the door of what looked like a beer joint, only then seeing a faded carved board behind a birdbath that assured us this was indeed Pee Wee's Place. Sometimes you just have to rely on your CBG instincts to tell you when you're there.

SOUTHERN MARYLAND

TOP OF THE HILL

15903 Marlboro Pike, east of Route 301 near Upper Marlboro, MD; phone: 301-627-2012.
C C C C G

Would You Get the Door Honey?

Now this is real barroom dining. Tables are an easy talking distance away from the bar and plenty of neon lights to help fade away any lingering glow of healthy suntan that patrons might be hiding. A place to keep up with the NASCAR race

schedule and all the country music you have been missing. A place for robust conversation, decent food, and a challenging pool table that offers home field advantage to the old customers.

And to think we might have missed it except for a rumor. First Spy Gale Waldron, (Lincoln, VA) said she thought she had seen a crummybutgood restaurant review in the *Washington Post* several years after my column had stopped. Curious, I searched, and found this quote in a review by *Post* writer Eugene Meyer: "From its looks, Top of the Hill would have been called 'Crummy But Good' under a rating system that was used in a former *Post* Food Section feature." When Eugene is right, he's right. Thank you, sir, for giving us Top of the Hill. I think we should make you an honorary Crummy But Good Scout.

First test at the Top of the Hill is whether you can open the door when it's closed tight. Fortunately, I had sent my wife ahead so I was spared the embarrassment of failing the jammed door challenge.

There is no test of the pocketbook. Prices are about as reasonable as you can get. My baked ham platter came with two thick slabs of decent ham. My companion's grilled cheese sandwich was pronounced perfect, especially when they added the fresh slice of tomato she requested. At one end of the bar, a female patron watched soap operas while the TV set at the other end offered sports and news. Something for everyone who loves a bar at Top of the Hill.

THE FRYING PAN RESTAURANT

East off Route 4, a few miles north of Solomons, at 9895 H.G. Trueman Road, Lusby, MD; phone: 410-326-1125.

C C G G G

On the Inside, Looking Inside

My CBG instincts told me that The Frying Pan was a good breakfast restaurant. Our efficient waitress agreed: "Can be hard to get a seat." But we were there for a late Friday lunch and the seating came easy. Still, my son's fresh swordfish special sandwich was the best six big bites of fish we tasted in Solomons country all weekend. My own fresh rockfish sandwich was a bit too sushi-like, a tad less grilled than the bread, but quickly consumed.

So good, that we did go back for breakfast and were not disappointed. Yes, the hash browns come in one large brown lump, but I have learned to go with the local hash brown flow. There is no single "right" way for hash browns. It's okay to harbor an inner favorite form of the fried potatoes, but otherwise, when in Rome enjoy them the Roman way. Isn't that one of the reasons to leave home and eat in Rome? Breakfast was good, served until 11:30, and the breakfast sandwiches were just under $3.00 (April 2002). You'll need those sandwiches as backup energy for exploring nearby Calvert Cliffs State Park, where the beach is home to fossil shark teeth. Finders, keepers.

First Fan Nick Brown (Lusby, MD) waxed romantic about his favorite CBG restaurant: "Located in Lusby's Government Center—that is, next to the (former) post office—The Frying Pan has that charm unique to vintage Butler Buildings. While its sign promises 'Steaks 'n Seafood,' it looks like it should be dispensing fertilizer and grass seed."

Within Nick's should-be feedstore, large picture windows separate the inner and outer dining rooms, as if the restaurant had grown like a tree and just added a new outer layer to accommodate the tourists. We sat with the tourists in the outer dining room and watched the regulars through the glass. We could see them talking but couldn't hear what they were saying. I had that aquarium feeling of staring at fish whose lips moved soundlessly while I nervously wondered if they were talking about me. Next time, I'm joining the regulars at the counter in the innermost layer. Then I'll look out through the glass at the surrounding tourists and say, "Read my lips."

CAPTAIN'S TABLE

275 Lore Road, tucked behind the well-hidden Comfort Inn, Solomons, MD; phone: 410-326-2772.
C C G G G

A Wisteria State of Mind

Sometimes it is easy to ignore the food and still pile up the good "G"s at a crummy restaurant. Good company, a dining

deck covered in wisteria overlooking Solomon's harbor at sunset, boats slipping past in the growing dark like twinkling Christmas trees on secret missions, a distant thunderstorm practicing for the Fourth of July. Who has time to waste worrying about the catch of the day?

Okay, the catch is usually pretty good, as is the crab soup. My constant companion—she who doesn't like fish but lets me drag her to endless shabby seafood places—enjoys the homemade meatloaf. She also enjoys with me backstreet places like the Captain's Table, where quiet moments are possible, conversation can be shared or not, and nobody notices thin rugs and plastic tablecloths. A loafing walk along the docks, a glass of wine, and thou. Tomorrow we can do the bustle side of the island.

WESTERN MARYLAND

NICK'S AIRPORT INN

Route 11 north of Hagerstown, MD, next to the airport; phone: 301-733-8560.
C G G

Best Mountainside Crab Cakes?

First Fan Virginia Strine (Hagerstown, MD) got right to the point. "Your crab cake article in the *Washington Post* this morning was all right, but the best crab cakes are made by my neighbor, Nick Giannaris, at the Airport Inn."

Nothing like the torrid praise of an "all right" to stir a writer's blood. Would you not rush to go on a blind date with someone described as "all right"? Despite the lukewarm praise, my constant companion and I happened to be in the Hagerstown area, and it was a good chance to prove my wise old saying about airport restaurants: Never eat there.

Me wrong, Virginia right. The broiled crab cake sandwich was the best crab cake I've had while nearly within sight of a mountain. Crisp outside, creamy inside, and filled with chunks of crab—the crab cake, not the mountain. Our waitress claimed that passengers at Hagerstown/Washington County International Airport often get crab cakes here to fly home with, and at least one company flies in about twenty employees just for an annual Christmas crab cake party.

On the downside, my companion's chicken breast sandwich looked great (topped with bacon, cheese, lettuce, and tomato), but was undercooked for our taste. Cooked chicken in the pink of health is a contradiction in terms.

But you can disregard everything I've said. Because Nick's Airport Inn just doesn't qualify as Crummy. Multiple forks and spacious dining rooms, including an extra-pleasant sunny porch, flower gardens, and excessive pink tablecloths—two tablecloths at dinner—push Nick beyond my normal Crummy beat. Even the view of the commercial backside of the airport seemed manicured compared to most airports.

My Crummy excuse is that we had to take this opportunity to admit to an exception to the "Never eat at an airport restaurant" rule. I suppose next I'll have to admit that some motel restaurants—like the Red Byrd—are edible too.

Red Byrd Restaurant and Motel
19409 Shepherdstown Pike (Route 34), Keedysville, MD, between Boonsboro and Sharpsburg, just north of Antietam National Battlefield; phone: 301-791-5915. C C G G G

The Waitress Who Had My Number

I believe we were discussing how wrong I can be. The last example being my wise old saying that airport restaurants are

the worst places to eat except for motel restaurants. And certainly, the wise but crummy traveler would never order crab cakes at a motel restaurant, no matter how much First Fan Richard McComb praised them.

For the record, I would have said something like Mrs. McComb told Richard: "For heaven's sake, don't order crab cakes here." The here being the Red Byrd Restaurant and Motel. While technically within the Chesapeake Bay drainage basin, it sure doesn't feel like Bay Country, like good crab country.

Ready to write off the Red Byrd quickly as just another bad motel restaurant, my constant companion and I ordered only a late afternoon dessert and coffee. She liked her "Original Red Byrd Cake," a light red velvet cake. But the pie's the thing.

Because the glazed peach pie was so fresh and good, we thought perhaps we should go ahead and try the luncheon meatloaf special (with two vegetables from a list of about ten choices). The meatloaf was good enough to push us into "just trying" the crab cakes (with roll and choice of two vegetables). For First Fan Richard McComb's sake, of course. Yes, Richard, the crab cakes were surprisingly good, but nothing to endanger our top ten list.

The Red Byrd serves breakfast all day during the week and

until 1 P.M. on weekends. This is also a good place to show the kids how bad the drapes at home would look if you crushed them behind the chairs for a million years.

The waitress was getting an obvious grin out of our continuous and backward food-ordering process. "Are you sure you're done and I can write up the bill?" she asked. I was too full to do anything but grunt a yes.

I sat back contented in my hiking shorts, crossed my legs, and rested a good cup of coffee against my bare bony knee at the table edge. Ah, middle age contentment. As the waitress kidded with us and tallied up the long dessert break turned lunch turned dinner, she also quietly and without explanation wrote something on my knee with her pen. My immediate male delusion of adequacy wondered if she had left me her phone number. Later examination revealed she had written two big zeroes. I hope that was not my final grade.

If this is not exactly top ten crab cake country, it is definitely top Civil War country. The Red Byrd lies just north of the Antietam battlefield. My favorite approach to Antietam is from Harpers Ferry north on Route 340 and then onto the Happy Valley road (Route 67) toward Boonsboro.

Driving north through the pleasant farm valley, it is easy to picture Confederate troops retreating west from Frederick, MD, through the passes on the valley's eastern ridge, across the valley bottom and over the next ridge toward Sharpsburg and the haven of Antietam Creek. The retreat of the Rebs is followed, but not too closely, by the Yankees. Farm wives and daughters stand at the fences of their stone farmhouses in the valley and provide drinks of cold water to the thirsty soldiers of both sides. As they drift west, the soldiers also liberate apples and green corn. The lush farm land still produces plentiful fruits and vegetables for the traveler who stops at the roadside stands or produce-filled pickup trucks.

The safest route to the Red Byrd Restaurant, Antietam, and Sharpsburg is to continue north through Happy Valley to the center of Boonsboro and then go south again on Route 34. But I cannot resist following the ghosts of the soldiers moving west across the distant low ridge. I'm drawn as they were out of Happy Valley, toward bloody Antietam, and usually end up wandering lost with the warrior ghosts on country roads.

BURKHOLDER'S BAKERY

106 East High Street, Sharpsburg, MD;
phone: 301-432-4145.
C G G G G

Where the Shoofly Pie Has a Wet Bottom

Should you wander south on Route 34 from the Red Byrd into Sharpsburg, a new addition to the CBG collection is this Mennonite-flavored bakery. Have a craving for wet-bottom shoofly pie? Or maybe it's been too long since your last fresh-picked rhubarb pie or still-warm loaf of spicy apple bread or peanut butter cookies, or . . . Well, you get the idea, and now you know where I head to try to satisfy those cravings, thanks to the advice of First Fan Laura Ellison.

Some baked goods are seasonal—like rhubarb pie and green tomato pie—and some—like buckeyes and apple dumplings—are made to order, so you might want to call ahead first. Yes, the place is kind of hard to find. (Turn east off Main Street onto Mechanic Street and drive two blocks, where you turn left onto High Street. The bakery is behind the big white house on the right.) And yes, it does kind of look like a bakery-in-the-garage-behind-the-house kind of place. And if all that is somehow too crummy for you, well then don't buy a bag of cookies and wander through the numerous back alleys of Sharpsburg. See if I care.

PARK-N-DINE RESTAURANT
Route 144, east end of Hancock, MD, off exit #3,
Route 70; phone: 301-678-5242.
C C G G G

The Deviled Eggs Made Me Do It

Actually, my editor made me do it. Like many travelers through western Maryland, her family has been stopping at the Park-N-Dine for years. Mine has too, but I didn't tell her that. Instead, I moaned and groaned about how much trouble it would be to go all the way out to Hancock just to check out her favorite place. I really made it sound like a tremendous sacrifice, but sometimes you have to do that with editors.

The Park-N-Dine has been feeding travelers since 1946, and it just keeps growing like Topsy. Or is it Turvy? On our last

visit, the afore-mentioned moan-and-groan trip, we sat in the oldest front section, which remains bright and intimate with a 1950s feel. Some of the tables in the newest, more cavernous section look out over the Potomac River and the C&O Canal. A fine view, if you can get it, but that day we couldn't.

The menu changes some from day to day and includes daily specials. On our Tuesday visit the menu showed five soups and forty-five dining selections. Plus twenty sandwiches, most priced under $2.50. And let's not forget the twenty vegetable side dishes, which include some hard-to-get selections like deviled eggs, butter beans, and boiled cabbage. No wonder travelers like to stop here—with about one hundred possibilities, even the fussiest kid should be able to find something. On the down side, the slow decision makers have 100 excuses to take forever. Thank goodness service is fast.

When in doubt, my constant companion always orders the veal parmigiana with spaghetti, which came out looking overdone, but tasted fine. I am always tempted by something I haven't had in a while, in this case the chef's special for the day, ham and oysters. On the same haven't-had principle, I made my two side dishes deviled eggs and green lima beans. The baked ham came with a dollop of red Jell-O and pineapple chunks, which I think was the chef's way of apologizing for the blandness of the ham. It needed something. Same with the deviled eggs. I say this knowing that I have been spoilt by too many summer picnics where my aunts tried to out devil each other's eggs. Each would try to fill her eggs with the richest, lightest, and most colorful filling. At the end of the picnic, they would quietly count who had the most eggs left on her platter. To the loser went the spoils. For my aunts, that's what it meant "to have egg on your face." Park-N-Dine wouldn't have a chance.

But that was then for maiden aunts and this is now for the busy traveler. Take a break from the road and see what has drawn locals and long-distance haulers alike to the Park-N-Dine for nearly sixty years. After all, this was my editor's choice and she did have enough good taste to make me her vegetable of the day.

BILL'S PLACE AND ORLEANS GROCERY

Sharp left at the bottom of Orleans Road, Little Orleans, MD. Take the Orleans Road exit south off U.S. I–68 about thirteen miles west of Hancock, MD; phone: 301-478-2701.
C C C C G G G

Forget the Minnow Bucket at Bill's Place

That Was Then: Sometimes you look at a place and just know you are going to have to wash in the minnow bucket. Otherwise you'll never pass as a regular. Why we have this obsession to look like we are a regular, local customer rather than a gawking tourist, I don't know. But if anyone can relax

you and make you feel at home, especially on an off-season day, then Bill of Bill's Place can.

From the outside, the old building looks like an abandoned feed mill with a high porch for unloading truckloads of grain. That's part of the "new" look added when the building was moved up the hill from the C&O Canal in 1904.

The sleeping hound on the porch gave my approach half an eyeball. Maybe his near ear quivered, but it sure didn't raise up any. Across the street was a canoe shed also marked "Bill's Place." But I headed for the larger building with the sign "Mayor's Office" and the step-over guard dog.

As my eyes adjusted to the darkness inside, I began talking to a raccoon sitting above the whiskey bottles at the counter/bar.

"What will you have?" asked the raccoon.

"Lunch," I said.

"Oh, I guess we can find something," Bill Schoenadel replied, as he and his cigar came out from behind the row of stuffed animals.

And with that Bill and I—mostly Bill—began a two-hour conversation that involved Colonel Cresap, Generals Braddock and Washington, President Grover Cleveland, printing presses, and the C&O Canal. Topics du jour included why Bill lost the post office in 1972 and an update on the fish-dipping war between the Feds and the locals. When Bill got too deep into a subject, his wife, Ethel, would quietly say, "That's enough, Bill." And Bill would dutifully change subjects.

In 1753, George Washington widened the nearby Cresap's Road on his way west to fight the French. He was badly defeated. Two years later, Washington joined Braddock in another expedition against the French. Again they widened the original road, and again they were defeated. There is something to be said for not widening the road less traveled.

But developers, even Colonial developers, never learned. Washington returned to push the building of the C&O Canal, which for a few prebankruptcy decades beat a commercial path past Little Orlean's door. The path has now been taken over by bikers, hikers and canoeists.

One legacy of the new towpath beaters is the collection of six thousand one-dollar bills customers have taped to the ceiling of Bill's Place. "They started doing that in '81," Bill said. "Stopped in '92. Just made the place too dark looking."

First Fan Norm Gunderson (Reston, VA) had steered me to Bill's Place. "My wife and I happen upon this place while hiking the C&O," Norm said. "Don't know if it was the hike, the mountain air, or the company, but a beer and cheeseburger never tasted better. Bill's Place was so Crummy But Good that we immediately thought of you."

Would-Be Fan Bruce Hopkins (Lincoln, VA) wrote to say, "I was just reading in a B&B newsletter about a ramshackled place in Little Orleans, MD, that serves great crab cakes. No name given. Sounds like your kind of place. I'm waiting to see what Mr. Crummy But Good has to say about it before venturing out to Little Orleans myself."

Sometimes food is secondary in a CBG restaurant. Bill's is such a place. But I dutifully asked if there was anything special for lunch. Bill turned to Ethel, his patient wife of fifty years, and asked, "What was that stuff you were serving yesterday?"

So I had yesterday's still decent Salisbury steak special. The menu—more map and history than food—tended toward the hearty hamburgers, soups, sandwiches, and big breakfasts that fuel the hunters, fishermen, Potomac River canoeists, and C&O hikers who are the bulk of Bill's customers. The locals rely on word of mouth to let them know about an unannounced fish fry or Saturday night jam session at Bill's. The rest of us have to depend on good timing.

And don't worry about washing in the minnow bucket. Bill, Ethel, and the step-over guard dog will take you just the way you are.

And This Is Now: Things change. First the step-over dog died. One of Bill's sons had him stuffed and mounted. For awhile, the step-over dog stood in a perpetual run behind the bar, chasing a stuffed rabbit like he hadn't done in years. Then the place burned down in November 2000, and not long after, Ethel died.

"We tried to keep the news of the fire from Ethel because she was so sick, but it was hard to do, what with the story being on CNN as well as the local news and papers. Finally the kids promised their mother they would build her a new apartment right away. But she said, 'Bill needs his bar first.' So here I am. Seventy-eight years old and starting over," Bill told me from behind his new bar.

Son Kevin built the yellow log structure and friends and neighbors pitched in. "Sure found out who my friends were and there are a lot of them," Bill said, still shaking his head in wonder. Hunters who stayed during the hunting season brought used bar stools, the American Legion threw a benefit dance, and rangers at the nearby state park took up a collection. People showed up with coolers, tables, and chairs. Patrons from across the country have contributed and written their names on about four hundred one-dollar bills that once again are beginning to cover the ceiling. The cheap and hearty menu is back and the fish sandwich has become the new favorite of the old-timers.

Above the bottled liquors, Kevin built a tin roof where water drips constantly and pleasantly before flowing off in a tin gutter. When I asked about the dripping water, Bill said with his old twinkle, "Makes it look like it's raining and we can't go fishing. Might as well hang out at the bar."

Things change, we lose friends and can't go home again. But sometimes stubborn people with extra grit like Bill insist that we join them in starting over and build a new crummybutgood home away from home.

BEST BBQ IN NORTHERN VIRGINIA IS...

DEAR FRIENDS OF CRUMMY BUT GOOD BBQ JOINTS . . .

When last we met, Reader Inge Collins was complaining of BBQ withdrawal symptoms. Seems her favorite crummybutgood place disappeared in a last bit of hickory smoke and she was looking for another good barbecue fix in Northern Virginia.

You CBG readers and scouts responded quickly, as always. And you may be right in your initial selections of the best BBQ places, just as you were when you picked "Most Likely to Succeed" back in high school. With such a proven track record, how could I not go along with the four places most highly recommended?

I even used some of your savvy comments to help make up a BBQ rating sheet to try to get us all nearly on the same page while we expand the quest for the ten best BBQ joints in the whole region, from the Blue Ridge Mountains of Virginia and West Virginia to the Bay Bridge in Maryland. The Great Crummy But Good BBQ Quest is on!

My two favorite barbecue places—Planet Wayside and

Ben's Whole Hog Barbecue—made the CBG top ten list and have already been reviewed. Ben's was by far the favorite among readers and scouts who voted in the initial round of the Best BBQ Quest, probably aided by a bit of Internet support that drew e-mail from fans as far away as Charlotte, NC.

Here are your choices for the next two closest-to-heaven CBG barbecue restaurants in Northern Virginia:

DIXIE BONES

134400 Occoquan Road, Woodbridge, VA; phone: 703-492-2205.
C C G G G

First Fan Karen Finkel (Fairfax Station, VA) found Dixie Bones all by herself, on the path from their sailboat to the laundromat, where she had gone "to wash some boat things. I was hungry and tired of hanging out in the laundromat, so I wandered next door and picked up the menu."

The rest is history. "We've taken many people there over the years, and 90 percent have liked it," Karen said, her own favorite being the catfish with the black lid barbecue sauce, Dixie chips extra crispy, and macaroni and cheese. Several fans sang in praise of the fried catfish, which I tried but was not driven to song. I will stick to the smoked meats on future visits.

My companion, a tough critic, thought her barbecued pork platter (with roll and two side dishes) lacked enough smoky taste, despite assurances that the meat had spent twelve to fourteen hours in the company of chain-smoking hickory logs. Toughie did praise the side dishes of coleslaw and baked beans and guarded carefully her slice of homemade coconut cream pie. Dixie featured at least six different made-from-scratch pies. By meal's end, Toughie was beginning to soften and chatting away with the owner about his display of bright Fiestaware plates from the 1950s.

BUBBA'S BAR-B-Q

7810-F Lee Highway, Arlington, VA;
phone: 703-560-8570.
C C G G G

With a name like Bubba's, who would expect sparkling white walls, healthy plants, and cute pig pictures? Methinks there is a Mrs. Bubba. Meknowso, because she was one of a bunch who e-mailed praise of the place.

First Fan Ellen Carpenter (Falls Church, VA) tempered her praise of Bubba's by saying, "It can almost hold a candle to the supreme arbiter of BBQ—Pierce's in Williamsburg." Ever notice how the BBQ sauce always drips better on the faraway side of the fence? Several readers referred to near-mythical faraway BBQ places. If we're lucky like Ellen, the sauce also drips pretty darn good close to home too. Her family particularly enjoys Bubba's takeout pulled pork barbecue by the pound. "Good enough to eat without sauce, a true sign of a great BBQ."

Several fans praised the Bubba fries, but we hit one of those cold and stale off days, definitely not a fries day. Two of us enjoyed our barbecue sandwiches. I think my brisket had more character, more smoke and bite, than her pulled pork.

The other companion turned out to be a ringer, actually a nonringer, a non-BBQ person. He complained bitterly about the slow service, until I reminded him that this was an order-at-the-counter place. Whereupon, he got up out of his seat and ordered a—Gasp!—cheeseburger. He tried to tell us how good it was, but we ignored him. Another candidate to be sent down to the crummybutgood farm team for retraining in BBQ appreciation.

I kidded our First Fan that Bubba's was short on the good-old-boy, flannel shirt atmosphere that was part of my BBQ upbringing. "What do you expect," she snorted back by e-mail, "you're inside the Beltway now."

She may be right. I guess when I want to wear flannel, trade barbs with the cook, and enjoy excellent barbecue too, I'll have to return to my own favorite BBQ places—somewhere beyond the Beltway in the land where even the ridges sing the blues.

The Crummy But Good Crab Cake War

ON STARTING A CRAB CAKE WAR . . .

It is so easy to start a war in Chesapeake Bay country. All you have to do is complete the following sentence: "The only place to get really good crab cakes is _____."

Wow. No other subject raises the passionate opinions of our Crummy But Good scouts more. They can really get their greasy chins up and out. Oh, a few completed the sentence with a note of family pride: "The only place to get really good crabcakes is in my kitchen/my mother's kitchen/at my aunt's in Baltimore." But most played by the rules and strongly recommended the crab cakes at some favorite Crummy But Good restaurant.

We checked out more than two dozen places that had received the most votes from readers or sounded most interesting and were within a two-hour drive of our favorite stomach pump. Which leaves some places unvisited. And we will get to them. Like the endless quest for the Holy Grill, for the perfect CBG restaurant, the search for the best crab cakes is never over.

To maintain our expected high scientific standards, we developed a special survey form and handpicked a crack crab cake team to join us in the testing. The combined average score of all testers is shown in parentheses at the start of each review. None of the crab cakes scored a perfect 25 and some missed it by a lot.

AND THE WINNERS ARE . . .

STONEY'S SEAFOOD HOUSE

Oyster House Road, Broomes Island, which is a left-hand turn near the end of Broomes Island Road, Route 264, which is a right-hand turn off Route 4, a few miles south of Prince Frederick, MD; phone: 410-586-1888 C G G G G (22.3 points)

Best All-Around Crab Cakes: Just Two Stoney Throws Away

Good crab cakes are more than just crabmeat, filler, and seasoning, just as a good kiss is more than the mere throwing together of four lips. The best crab cakes came wrapped in a special feeling that said, "Welcome to Chesapeake Bay country. We make crab cakes the right way—our way." Although we gave 80 percent of our review grades to the crab cakes that were set before us, the remaining 20 percent covered the total dining experience, which helped measure the step up from mere good food to a great eating experience.

First Fan Eddie Becker (Silver Spring, MD) said, "If you know

about a crab cake that is better than Stoney's at Broomes Island, MD, then I want to know about it." We don't. Stoney's did the best at bringing everything together: excellent crab cakes, tables that overlook the water, a wait staff eager to serve, fun, peaceful location on a working waterfront where fresh crabs are docked daily, and an entertaining mixture of tourists and locals, from weekend boaters in shorts and black business socks to watermen in proud sweat.

I took my crab cake sandwich broiled (with coleslaw and market priced). It came out huge, nicely crusted on the outside and creamy on the inside. The pan-fried cakes were equally good. A four-ounce baby crab cake sandwich is also available. Two companions did wish for a sharper taste of Old Bay Seasoning, but the rest of us happily munched on.

But does Stoney's qualify as Crummy? Another Fan, Melissa McCormick (Solomons, MD), proclaimed Stoney's "the only crab cake that exists in Southern Maryland . . . and the place isn't crummy, it's casual. You know, a pull-up-in-your-boat-and-bathing-suit-type place." Some who pulled up in bathing suits should have worn a boat, but that's part of the fun.

We decided that Stoney's qualified for at least one "C" just because the Patuxent River had battered away enough spit and polish to show who's boss. And because enough passing bathing suits revealed bodies whose temple days were numbered.

Stoney's has recently added another waterfront location, in Solomons (as you head south on Route 4, turn left onto Dowell Road at the fire station on your left towards the Calvert Marina; phone: 410-326-1036). Although the two waterfront locations close during the winter, the dry dock location with the fireplace remains open year-around (545 Solomons Island Road North, Prince Frederick, MD; phone: 410-535-1888).

G&M RESTAURANT

804 North Hammonds Ferry Road, Linthicum, MD;
phone: 410-636-1777.
C C C G G G G   (20.0 points)

Best Nearby Cake Port in Any Storm

When the weather is too hot, too cold, or too wet to sit outside, or when you find yourself closer to BWI Airport or the Beltway than Broomes Island, then try the crab cakes at G&M. This is where the first shot in the Great Crab Cake War was fired, when Ann Moses (Silver Spring, MD) convinced me that it was the only place to go for crab cakes. To quote me: "Excellent. And so meaty as to belong in the heavyweight class of crab cakes without filler." Or as Second Fan Peter Marx (Annapolis, MD) lamented,

"Okay, when my mother visits, I'll probably take her to Stoney's. But I'll be talking about G&M."

You can also blame my daughter for getting me hooked on G&M crabcakes. Somewhere in the Father's Manual, Virginia Edition, it says that fathers must get up at 2:30 in the morning to drive their daughters seventy-five Beltway miles to BWI Airport. (See Chapter 2, "Fathers Can't Say No to Their Daughters, So Don't Even Try.") The only other good reason to go to BWI is the crab cakes at G&M Restaurant, about five miles away in Linthicum, MD. (Virginians: say "Lin," mumble a couple of syllables, and end in a strong "UM" sound. Or, if you are of the diehard Confederate persuasion, say "Lee to come!" real fast.)

My new crab cake buddy Ann Moses (Silver Spring, MD) wrote to warn me that the "outside of this place is something else." It certainly is, especially when I arrived from BWI so dim early in the morning. Even the work crew seemed to be afraid to go into the G&M Restaurant. Turned out they were just standing around, waiting for the boss, who was late with the key, but the dubious impression remained.

One does not just order crab cakes at the crack of daylight, even in Maryland. I started with what the menu board called a Gree omelet. My first bite exploded on an unexpected bit of peppercino. My next several bites were quickly into toast chased by water. Suddenly very awake, I and the omelet got along fine after that as we shared a pleasant combination of eggs, onions, black and brown olives, green peppers, and feta cheese.

The big wake-up omelet and constant coffee refills gave me time and energy to plead with Karen Cabe, my early morning cashier/waitress. Had I not traveled seventy-five miles from far-off Virginia just for their famous crab cakes? Please don't ask me to wait until 11 A.M., the normal start of the crab cake hours. Karen and the cook relented. They agreed to put together a broiled crab cake platter to go.

The five-booth take-out area made chatting with strangers easy. As I waited for my crab cakes, at least five different regular customers smacked unsolicited lips on behalf of the treat awaiting me: "Unfreaking believable" was roughly what they said.

They were right. The G&M crab cakes traveled well back to Virginia, where I broiled and reheated them gently for supper. Excellent. And so meaty as to belong in the heavyweight class of crab cakes without filler.

For the record, G&M serves other foods and has other seating areas, but Ann Moses and I can't help you much with the rest of the menu. There is a good reason why G&M serves three to four thousand pounds of crabmeat a week. And that's reason enough for us.

And now we Virginians know why Marylanders put BWI Airport so close to unpronounceable Lin . . . UM. Have crab cakes, will travel.

CAPTAIN BILLY'S CRAB HOUSE

Pope's Creek, MD, about seven miles south of La Plata, right-hand turn off Route 301; phone: 301-932-4323. C C G G G (19.5 points)

A Bridge and a Booth

A nice setting overlooking the Potomac River in a quiet part of southern Maryland is worth a couple of "G"s. The restaurant does seat four hundred and can get crowded. Crowded is an entertaining plus for some, a distracting minus for others. Crab cakes were good, although a bit bland and not quite lumpy enough for us. But the coleslaw and especially the corn fritters

were worth fighting over. Most patrons come to eat off brown butcher paper and cast crab shells to the four winds. John Wilkes Booth came to nearby Dents Meadows to borrow a boat and sneak off to Virginia. Guess he couldn't wait for the Route 301 Bridge that now gracefully crosses the distant background.

JERRY'S SEAFOOD

9364 Lanham Severn Road, Seabrook, MD, just east of the Beltway; phone: 301-577-0333.
C C G G G (19 points)

Dear Expense Auditor:

Derrick made me do it. He said I had to try the most expensive crab cake yet. How could I not when Derrick Damions (Greenbelt, MD) double dog dared me: "I grew up in a Chesapeake family and have had my share of Maryland c cakes and such, but Jerry's cakes are called BOMBS and they will blow u away." So did the price. The Baby Bomb provides

a cheaper starter kit to help you decide if you want to bomb away. Also available at lunch, a more modest crab cake sandwich that scored a 19 and a Jerry-trademarked spicy firecracker crab cake entrée with bread and two side dishes.

After the last Crab War, Second and Third Fans Jerry and Marion Lane rechecked G&M, Billy's, and Jerry's for us and declared, "We think the Crab Bomb at Jerry's is in a classification by itself!" I think that's a positive endorsement, but I remember a long-ago blind date who was also described as "in a classification by herself." I still wake up screaming in the night, and the worst part is that she dumped me.

In addition to the award for Most Expensive Crab Cake, Jerry's won Best Service. I was amazed to pull into yet another drab shopping center at 2 P.M. on a Wednesday afternoon and find a line of fifteen people waiting patiently in the hot sun to get into this modest-looking restaurant. Jerry himself came out to serve us free shrimp appetizers.

Despite the crowded restaurant, the waitress took my order immediately. Because I was planning to taste, doggy-bag, and run, I told her to forget the tempting basket of warm bread. Not to be. First another waitress and then Jerry himself brought me bread and each apologized for it not being there. I felt important. Broke, but important.

CANTLER'S RIVERSIDE INN
458 Forest Beach Road, exit 28 off Route 50 and then a bunch of turns, near Annapolis, MD; phone: 410-757-1467.
C C C G G   (18 points)

Just a Bobbin' On

We arrived by water. On the way Captain Peter Marx had to dodge Coast Guard boats, which were busy setting up traffic cones in the river. Seems the president was speaking at the Naval Academy. The final water approach to Cantler's was framed nicely by the hulks of two old boats, sitting low in the water like two old retired men, each bobbing on about their yesterdays. Today's story was the dock at Cantler's crawling with bushels of crabs being sorted into holding tanks.

All of which built up expectations that made the not-quite-perfect freshness of the crab cakes doubly disappointing. Our waiter assured us that the crab cakes were made fresh every morning, but on our visit that longed-for crabby sweetness in a fried cake was missing. We will be back. Too many readers have praised Cantler's menu, and it's just too enjoyable a location not to try again.

DAVIS' PUB

400 Chester Avenue, Eastport–Annapolis, MD; phone: 410-268-7432.
C C C G G (18 points)

A Sailor's Port

The neighborhood hangout with a jukebox and much favored by our Annapolis team. Although the crab cakes lacked the lump meat we normally seek, the team voted these the best non-lump cakes yet. First Fan Kate Naughten said, "French fries were great, coleslaw forgettable, and local sailors plentiful."

ANGLER'S RESTAURANT AND MARINA

**3015 Kent Narrows Way, Grasonville, MD;
phone: 410-827-6717.**
C C C C G G (16 points)

Bay Bridge Break

Sometimes you cross over on the Bay Bridge in a slow sea of taillights and immediately wonder "Why?" When "Ocean City" no longer seems a good enough answer, here's a safe back-home harbor for pondering such eternal questions, while turning over actual command to a crew of waitresses who still call you "Honey."

Like First Fan Betty Hayes (Alexandria, VA), I was first lured to Grasonville by the call of the too not-so-crummy Narrows Restaurant across the street. But I feel much more at home at Angler's. Crabcakes were pretty good and came in two sizes: a large lump crab-cake sandwich and a smaller not-so-lump version. Go for the large lumps.

OLIVE GROVE

**705 North Hammonds Ferry Road, Linthicum, MD;
phone: 410-636-1385.
C G G (16 points)**

So Close, So Far

So close to G&M Restaurant, but yet so far. Admittedly, we got off on the wrong foot. Or the hostess did, when she led us two steps toward our table and then abandoned us for a ringing phone. Two customers in hand should be worth more than one ringing phone in the bush. Still, First Fan Sheila Holzberger and family come here often, all the way from Frederick, MD. "The Olive Grove's crab cakes hardly have any filler in them— they're real crab. Plus, they come with all-you-can-eat salad and breadsticks, as well as a side of pasta."

If your date is frightened off by the outside appearance of G&M, then the Olive Grove is a good plan B.

JOE'S OCEAN COVE

**near Winchester, VA, about two miles south of Route 50 on Route 522; closed Mondays; phone: 540-662-9636.
C C C G G G (16 points)**

Dear Virginia, Dear D.C.: Try Harder

We visited more than half a dozen reader-recommended places in Virginia, and a ninth-place finish overall by Joe's was the best the state could do, unless we want to talk proudly

about the last-place finisher. On the other hand, we didn't get a single nomination for a place in Washington, DC. Is there not a crab cake worth its Old Bay Seasoning inside the Washington Beltway or in Northern Virginia?

Meanwhile, back in Stonewall Jackson Country, we visited Joe's Ocean Cove, south of Winchester. "Are you Joe?" I asked the wispy old man who got up from the bar and slowly approached our table with menus.

"What's left of me," said Joe Bugaski. His grin grew while the rest of him seemed to get even thinner. Joe's fifty-year campaign to bring good seafood to the northern Shenandoah Valley would have worn out Stonewall Jackson himself.

And this is Jackson Country. Pictures of Jackson and Robert E. Lee share the wall with some other fighters—John F. Kennedy, Harry S Truman in Mason garb, Rocky Marciano, and Carmen Basillio—as well as the expected dusty ships and long-stuffed fish.

Joe looked like he might have once been a fighter himself. "Did you know these boxers?" I asked.

"No," said Joe, growing younger as he talked, "I just collect pictures."

Not all mysteries should be explained on the first few visits. We plan to go back. My fried seafood platter was good, especially considering that the ocean was several blue ridges away.

Joe's son Victor—"I've only been here twenty-five years"—said that they make their own crab cakes and batter and fry the fish, shrimp, and scallops fresh each day. My nonseafood-loving constant companion (aka wife Rita) enjoyed her spaghetti—"on the sweet side, like your mother makes." She said she looked forward to coming back, something she has never said before about a seafood place.

First Fan Frank Wright (Fairfax, VA) accurately noted, "Joe's Cove is right out of the 1950s! As the fluorescent lights wore out, Joe replaced them with low-wattage bulbs, making the place dim and dimmer except for the bright old jukebox."

This is not lump crab cake country, but our Blue Ridge team stands like a stone wall in their loyalty to Joe's version.

TIMBUKTU RESTAURANT AND LOUNGE

1726 Dorsey Road, Hanover, MD;
phone: 410-768-4331.
C C C G G (5.6/11.8 points)

The Mystery of It All

Because Timbuktu received the most votes from our readers, we confidently went there to launch the Great Crab Cake War. It turned into the First Battle of Bull Run (Yankee version) all over again (final score 5.6). A full charge to the rear.

Team members Ann and Pat had been to Timbuktu about ten times before for crab cake sandwiches. This day, Ann and Pat said, was definitely the worst. Annapolis Eastsider Peter commented, "A very eggy taste smacks you in the face." The high

point for Annapolis teammate Kate was playing with the blue camels that decorate the bedraggled and bedecorated outside of Timbuktu. Her recommendation: "Don't go back unless they offer free camel rides."

But because of the large popular vote, we felt compelled to give Timbuktu a second chance, and even enlisted repeat visits by ardent Timbuktu fan Ron Works (Bethesda, MD). Results: The cakes doubled in score (11.8), but still underwhelmed most of us. Everyone was impressed with the size and appearance of the crab cakes, but agreed they didn't taste as good as they looked.

In Crabby Conclusion

And what about all the other crab cake places that didn't quite make our top ten list? Some general comments from our reviewers:

- Back off on the filler and let the fresh crabmeat speak for itself.
- Taste your own cooking: too often the crab cakes looked good, smelled good, and were even easy to dance to, but awful disappointing to eat.
- We know you are in a hurry, but don't microwave the rolls.
- Run a grouchy server check and avoid woefully forgettable service.

Gaining entrance to crab cake heaven requires more than flipping a burger that happens to be crabmeat. If your favorite crummybutgood restaurant promises to keep trying, so will we.

SOME CRAB CAKE RECIPES

Our reviewers ranged in background from raw Blue Ridge innocence to the salty toughness of east side Annapolis. After intensive training, they were even more unmanageable. Part of the team blindly compared some favorite take-out restaurant crab cakes against some favorite homemade recipes. To be fair, all crab cakes were prepared ahead of time and reheated for the testing.

The top three were

- (17.6) Takeout crab cakes from G&M Restaurant
- (16.2) Kimberley's Decadent Crab Cakes
- (13.9) Barbara and the Captain's Crab Cake Mix (commercial mix)

Although G&M would not share their recipe with us, Kimberley and Barbara were willing.

Kimberley's Decadent Crab Cakes

Kimberley Taylor (Arlington, VA), the token professional fooder on our team, describes herself as "a chef, who specializes in pastry." So what are crab cakes if not the Bay's special pastry?

8 OUNCES JUMBO LUMP BLUE CRAB
8 OUNCES BACKFIN BLUE CRAB
   (IT'S BEST IF THE CRABMEAT HAS NEVER BEEN FROZEN)
2 EGGS
1/2 CUP GOOD-QUALITY MAYO
DASH OF WORCESTERSHIRE SAUCE
1 TEASPOON DIJON MUSTARD
1/2 TEASPOON LEMON ZEST

5–8 SLICES GOOD-QUALITY WHITE BREAD (bread with some body to
   it; no air bread, please)

HANDFUL OF FRESH PARSLEY, MINCED

BUNCH OF FRESH CHIVES, SNIPPED

SALT AND PEPPER

GOOD-QUALITY SWEET BUTTER, CLARIFIED, FOR SAUTÉING (I used
   Plugra, because it contains less water and is best quality)

Carefully sort through the crabmeat for shell, being careful not
to smush the meat. In a food processor, turn the white bread,
sans crusts, into bread crumbs. Break eggs into a bowl and
lightly whisk them. Whisk in the mayo, Dijon, zest, a dash of
salt and pepper (to taste), and Worcestershire. Place some but
not all of the bread crumbs atop the crabmeat. Carefully pour
some but not all of the egg mixture atop that. Gently incorpo-
rate the mixture. If you like your crab cakes wet, add more liq-
uid; like it dry, add more crumbs. The goal is everything holding together nicely, without being too wet or dry. Save some
bread crumbs for the coating.

Now add herbs, blending lightly. Form the crab mix into
balls, patting them slightly flat with your hands (about 1/2 to
3/4 cup each). Take the remaining bread crumbs and liberal-
ly coat the outside of the cakes, and then set the cakes on a
tray to rest. Refrigerate for at least an hour, but overnight is
great.

Heat a large skillet with clarified butter. When it's good and
hot but not smoking, carefully place the cakes in the pan, trying to keep them separated, and gently shake the pan so the
cakes don't stick to it. Quickly sauté them, till they're golden on
each side, while shaking the butter around so they all get plenty. Serve immediately, garnished if you like with lemon wedges
and tartar sauce (or better yet . . . remoulade).

To clarify butter, melt at a very low heat. When completely
melted, skim the white fat off the top (if any has floated up).

Then carefully spoon out the yellowish oily part, being careful to leave the white solids on the bottom of the pan. The purpose of doing this is so that you can use the butter at a higher temperature (with its solids, butter burns at a much lower temperature). Sautéing at a higher temperature allows the outside to sear and caramelize a bit, while not absorbing too much of the fat. Cooked at a lower temperature, the crab cake would act like a sponge and taste oily.

Yield 6–8 nice size cakes or a dozen and a half "crab balls."

Barbara and the Captain's Crab Cake Mix

Barbara Herring (Vienna, VA) won our #1 Crab Cake Scout Award for hosting our recipe tasting, doing all the reheating, as well as preparing several recipes for us. The most popular of these was a commercial mix—Captain's Crab Cake Mix— from Crab Express, Salisbury, MD (1-800-CRAB-MIX). The mix had been first recommended to us by a shy member of the Chesapeake Yacht Club, who really wanted us to review the Captain's Gallery in Crisfield, MD. "We all adore the crab cakes there. You may also order the mix by phone. One of the secrets that I have found is to buy the backfin crab meat, and to mix the ingredients in ever so gently," she shyly said.

1 POUND CRABMEAT.
1 BOX OF CAPTAIN'S CRAB CAKE MIX

Put contents of dry mix in a mixing bowl. Add the packet of special mix. Blend in one pound of crabmeat. Let the mixture sit in the refrigerator for at least twenty minutes. Form into crab cakes and fry or broil until golden brown.

GONE BUT NOT FORGOTTEN

Once upon a time, Tyrannosaurus Rex and his friends ruled the earth. But asteroids happen. So it is with CBG restaurants. Here today, too often gone tomorrow. Sometimes we lose our crummybutgood friends in the big bang of a grease fire or the wrecking ball of new development. More often they are nibbled down by Mc-competition or old age or rising taxes or deteriorating facilities.

But these old friends and favorite places live on in our memories, faintly remembered ghosts of the past, like your second kiss or your junior prom date, that can still bring a smile to your lips.

In a larger sense, we cannot hallow, cannot honor, these brave crummy restaurants, living and dead, that struggled here to feed us. The outside world will little note nor long remember what we ate here, but we few can never forget the special joy they brought here. It is for us, the crummybutgood survivors, rather, to be dedicated to the unfinished food and company they have thus far so nobly advanced. It is for us to resolve that crummybutgood restaurants of the people, by the people, and for the people shall not perish from Earth.

And if you can't swallow all that, tough. I'm going to go ahead and share some memories of several of my favorite places that vanished during the past decade.

125

BUTTERMILK CAFÉ

formerly at 306 N. Talbot Street, which is Route 33 and the main drag, St. Michaels, MD.
C C G G G

Daze of Vine and Thunder

Our second greatest fear was that the wild vines would get us. Coils of morning glory twined around us on the dining deck and a twisted band of wisteria and mad roses reached over the fence, growing faster than the gardener could hack them back. The whole garden was like that, given into midsummer madness, tall weeds running amuck in the beds of spiky purple flowers, looking like wild barbarians sacking royal Rome. My kind of garden: Crummy But Good, full of life, ignoring rules.

But our first greatest fear was not being able to clean our plates, which could bring down the wraith of the owners. Louise and Douglas Taylor were like two old disheveled thunder clouds drifting through the cafe, always looming on the horizon with more food. Good-hearted thunder clouds, ones that had been bumping into each other and their dining patrons for so many years that they had nothing left to prove and coddled no prisoners. They thundered and struck as the mood fitted them, dunder and blitzen providing a refreshing change from the schlock and klitch that infect some parts of touristy St. Michaels.

First Fan Derek Rhymes had warned us. "The cafe is in a plain old house slightly away from the downtown St. Mike's hustle. You wouldn't even know it's a cafe if there weren't a sign saying so. You walk in the front door into an old living room that has three or four tables. Furniture doesn't match, no hostess/waiter/waitress to be seen. Probably nobody else in the joint," Derek said. "If you walk into the kitchen and give a 'Helllloooooo,' one of them will pop out eventually." Which is exactly what happened.

The food was good, and in the words of the beleaguered gardener, "Anyone who leaves here hungry, it's their own fault." Each day the Taylors post a new menu of about four entrées that come in lunch- and dinner-size packages. "Don't print any menus because we cook fresh every day," the Mrs. huffed.

Our dinners started with a homemade campanata relish. When asked for the main ingredient, the Mr. said, "It's eggplant, I hate to tell you." As if we would turn up our noses in the presence of eggplant. The campanata was followed by chunks of fresh melon on toothpicks and hot popovers that the Mr. grumbled were "more trouble than they were worth."

He picked fresh mint from the garden for our iced tea, tall sprigs that tickled our noses twice—first with the minty aroma and then by direct tickling touch. The salads were super fresh and piled with tomatoes and mushrooms. My crab cake dinner (with boiled young potatoes, broccoli, and two ears of corn-on-the-cob, $13.95) was big and meaty, the outside fried an unusual chocolate brown, the inside creamy and lightly stained with Worcestershire sauce and mustard. "I use just a touch of crumbled saltine crackers, but it's mostly meat and sautéed in butter, as it should be," the Mrs. said.

My constant companion's chicken fillets (with same vegetables, $8.95) were not as good as my crab cake. A bit tough, and somehow untouched by the good mushroom sauce that I helped her finish. "What can I say. Chicken is boring," Mrs. Taylor said. "Try something more exciting next time."

You can feel the Long Island influence, where the Taylors once lived and where they ran a large restaurant, Yale Barns, in Connecticut, that earned three stars from the *New York Times*. The Mrs. also cooked for some prominent families, including Governor Nelson Rockefeller and the heirs to the Seagram empire. The Mr. talked about long years working in the Long Island gas tank fields before returning to the restaurant business and catering.

We could not leave without admiring the paintings and hooked rugs that Mrs. Taylor has produced over the years. Mr. Taylor grumbled about the constant long hours his "Boss" demanded. "We're not retired, we're retarded." He tried hard not to show his pride in her work. Two full lives that have already left many happily full patrons in their thundering wake.

HENKEL'S RESTAURANT

formerly at 8955 Henkel's Lane, Annapolis Junction, MD; see complicated directions below.
C C C C G G G

"H" Is for Henkel's, "I" Is for Extra-Interesting

We rode up to the rickety old saloon at sunset. The building looked its age—about 150 years and many battles old. I expected to see Bad Bart the outlaw and his six guns waiting for me, maybe on the roof behind the false storefront or behind the railing that protected nothing on the second-floor balcony.

I walked boldly into the dim interior, and in my best John Wayne voice said, "Where's the bartender?"

"Right here, it's all hard wood," said Maury Amsterdam. "You might try the pine railing down at the end. It looks softer."

That kind of place. Kidding waiters: atmosphere by the bucket; dark, dusty corners; old photos begging for captions; construction workers in sweaty T-shirts; train commuters with ties just loosened; large families bumping together. We gave Henkel's an extra "I" for being extra-Interesting.

When I finally found the bartender, he told me that Henkel's has been a bar and restaurant since the 1840s, when it was a stop on the East Coast version of the Pony Express. The former post office now hides behind a dartboard. Photographs on the wall show patrons in front of the already rickety building in the 1860s. Bad Bart is the mean-looking guy on the left.

First Fan Ron Work (Bethesda, MD) said, "It's hard to find a larger sandwich. And it will be difficult to eat at a fast food place again." He's right. My companion chewed and walked around her "Henkel's Famous Ham through the Garden Sandwich" for half an hour and never could finish it. This was one time when, in the war between quantity and quality, both sides seemed to win. Except for the good cole-slaw, I didn't have near as much fun with my Special (Henk-L-Burger served on white bread with French fries and Grandmother's secret gravy and homemade coleslaw). I asked the waiter about desserts. He looked at me funny and said, "I'll have to check. After our sandwiches, nobody ever asks for dessert."

The trains are another draw. The kids at the table next to mine rushed out every time they heard the rumble. I did too. But be careful: the tracks seem nervously close and open.

Second Fan Leo Lemley (Potomac, MD) said Henkel's "fast became the favorite lunch and watering hole for most of the analysts and crypys at the National Security Agency . . . at least the ones who wanted to stay sane."

Good news: "They put paneling and a new ceiling in a few years ago so that 'special seasoning' does not fall on your food when trains rumble past," reported Third and Fourth fans, Mike and Jackie Egan (Brookeville, MD).

Bad news: the restroom water. When we were there, a sign on the sink simply said, "Contaminated Water." I talked to the manager, who assured me that they use bottled water for all cooking and drinking. The questionable water from the local well is used just for cleaning.

A second drawback is that you can't get there from here. It's almost easier to go by train. If you do make it there, Henkel's gives you a map to help you find your way home. On our first try to find the place, we ended up in a rock quarry, but could clearly see Henkel's, unreachable, across the railroad tracks. Fifth Fan Pat Campbell (Annapolis, MD) offered these directions: The restaurant is located off Route 32 between the Baltimore–Washington Parkway and Route 1. From the Parkway, take Route 32 West and exit on Dorsey Run Road, turn left, cross over 32 and make first left on Henkel Lane. The restaurant is past the Savage Rail Station, at the end of Henkel Lane.

See you in the rock quarry. Watch out for Bad Bart. He may be hiding behind that ham sandwich at the next table.

PAISANOS RESTAURANT
formerly 433 North Frederick Avenue, Gaithersburg, MD.
C C C G G G

Pat on the Belly, No Charge

Where I grew up, strangers do not pat grown men on their stomachs and say, "Did you enjoy the meal?" But Mr. Mike does. Mike Azat, the seventy-year-old owner and barkeep at Paisanos, has that lean and weathered twinkle of universal grandfathers who are allowed to do anything. Patrons tell me he gardens all day to grow the vegetables used in the restaurant, and then he barkeeps all night to help his customers grow. Sounds like a stretch, but I believe them.

The exterior of the restaurant is not quite as friendly as Mr. Mike himself. Not so much crummy as foreboding in the winter dark, a weathered pueblo bunker fortress with strange angles and nooks.

Inside was jolly enough. Tables for thirty-two parties of four, except when it rains hard and the fortress leaks and four tables become puddles. We ordered the favorite meals of our waitress—French Quarter Fettuccini ($9.95) and Chicken Marsala ($8.50)—and were quite pleased. Homemade sauces and salad dressings added to the freshness.

In trying to describe the interior decor, First Fan Mathina Carkci said, "I used to waitress there and got a kick out of watching customers laugh and point out all the oddities to one another." Good food, a laugh, and a free grandfatherly pat on the belly. What more can one ask of a restaurant?

ACKNOWLEDGMENTS

The sad news is all the favorite crummybutgood restaurants and haunts we have lost and the many that remain endangered by the encroachment of nonnative chain restaurants and the alarming tendency of those that would be rich and beautiful to look down their long noses at those comfortable bits of native backstreet Americana that many of us love.

The happy news is the growing company of Crummy But Good Scouts and Companions who are determined to find, visit, and support all the good eating places that happen to be crummy. To these people, this written record of the ongoing Quest for the Holy Grill is dedicated. Without you, this book would not exist. I have long hesitated to make a list of your names, because I know I have forgotten, misplaced, and misspelled many. Most I know only through the magic of e-mail. Sadly, this means I know some of the best Scouts only as flickering screen names that ran briefly and coldly across my computer screen. In addition, several dozen brave Companions have joined me as dining partners to test the merits of recommended places, and some of these I remember only as good company and not as names.

So I hesitate to present the following list of official Crummy But Good Scouts, Companions, and Advisers because at best it is incomplete. But it is the nature of these Scouts to quickly let me know when they think I have gotten something wrong, so why not in the Acknowledgments section too? To all those good Scouts named and not, my thanks.

To that special inner circle of family, friends, enemies, companions, and editors who deserve special thanks, I hope you know who you are and have already received a hug or a shoulder punch of appreciation. Because I'm going to stop writing now. There's this great Crummy But Good place that I just heard about and . . .

Known Crummy But Good Scouts, Companions, and Advisers

Madeline Albright (Planet Wayside), Maury Amsterdam (Henkel's), Jan Arneson (Vienna Inn), Diane Atkins (Cafe Monti), Barry (Bar-J), Eddie Becker (Stoney's), George Berklacey (Companion), Lawrance Binda (Banducci's), Helen Blackwell (Blue Ridge Seafood), John Wilkes Booth (Captain Billy's), Ken Briers (Barbara Fritchie), Pat Campbell (Henkel's), Walter Campbell (Lauder's), Barbara Cantor (Moon Cafe), Mathina Carkci (Paisano's), Ellen Carpenter (Bubba's Bar-B-Q), Sounia Nejad Chaney (doo gheh advisor), Phil Cohen (Companion, deli adviser), Inge Collins (BBQ alerts), Derrick Damions (Jerry's Seafood), Jim Devine (Companion), Mike and Jackie Egan (Henkel's), Laura Ellison (Burkholder's Bakery, granddaughter Alice), Karen Fairweather (Barbara Fritchie), Karen Finkel (Dixie Bones), Jack Fischer (Taste of the World, Companion), Frank Forrester (Thelma's Home Made Ice Cream, Companion), David Furst (radio guy, Companion), Mary Gallagher (Dee Dee's), Norm and Katherine Gunderson (Bill's Place), Trudy Harlow (Companion), Betty Hayes (Angler's), Andrea Louise Heggen (Ercilia's), Barbara Herring (crabcake host,

ACKNOWLEDGMENTS

Companion), Sheila Holzberger (Olive Grove), Bruce Hopkins (Bill's Place, Companion), Nancy Hughes (Warrenton Plaza), "Michigan Jack" (Havabite Eatery), Stonewall Jackson (Joe's Ocean Cove), D. J. Janik (Waffle Shop), Bettie Kahn (Ercilia's), Carol Kaltenbaugh (Havabite Eatery), Judy Karpinski (Park-N-Dine, enthusiastic editor), Esther Kelly (biggest fan, back patter, tail kicker), Kathleen Kelly (Bon Matin, granddaughter Isabella), Mike Kelly (Companion, granddaughter Alice), Rita Kelly (Constant Companion, other biggest fan), Jerry and Marion Lane (Jerry's Seafood), Frank and Henrietta Leimbach (Nick's Diner), Leo Lemley (Henkel's), Patricia Levine (Havabite Eatery), Terry Light (Ben's Whole Hog), Ken and Mary Ellen Lowery (Companions), Bob Luce (Payne's Biker Bar), Peter Marx (G&M, boat captain, Companion), Richard McComb (Red Byrd), Melissa McCormick (Stoney's), Jerry McCoy (Tastee Diner), Mike McDermott (Companion), Karole and Diehl McKalip (Companions), Chuck McKeon (Angie's), Nancy McKeon (Great First Editor), Eugene Meyer (Top of the Hill), Phil Million (Quarterdeck), Ann Moses (G&M), Pat Nash (Angie's), Kate Naughten (Moon Cafe, Davis's Pub, vegan consultant), Dan Noble (Topside Inn), Diane Noserale (Blue Ridge Seafood), Jane Perry (Barbara Fritchie), Rae Phillips (Whitey's), Rebecca Phipps (Blue Ridge Seafood), Ted Preisser (Shamshiry), Hilary Ray (Charcoal Kabab), Caroline Reutter (Pee Wee's Place), Derek Rhymes (Buttermilk Cafe), Lori Sampson (Mayur Kabab House), Steve Scafidi (Fran's Place, granddaughter Isabella), Helen Schmid (Cafe Monti), Neil Scott (Bistro Italiano), Gayle Sisler (Companion), Mitch Snow (Mom's Apple Pie Company, Li Ho, Companion, Latin America adviser), Candy Staulcup (illustrator who makes me look good), Virginia Strine (Nick's Airport Inn), Kimberley Taylor (crab cake cook), Patti Tuholski (Vienna Inn), Tyrannosaurus Rex (Gone But Not Forgotten), Mike Walker (Waffle Shop), Neal O. Weigel (Silver Diner), Gail

Wendt (Companion), Eric Wenocur (Moby Dick House of Kabob), Cathy Wine (Li Ho), Ron Works (Timbuktu, Henkel's), Frank Wright (Joe's Ocean Cove), and Lou Yost (Vienna Inn, Companion).

YOU TOO CAN BE A CRUMMY BUT GOOD SCOUT

Heck, you probably already are a crummybutgood scout. Why else would you read all the way to the end of this book?

Except it's not the end, and that's the beauty of the quest. We can each continue the quest for the holy grill, for the perfect crummybutgood restaurant, right up until the time our grandchildren are cutting up our food for us and nobody knows if we are drooling out of pleasure or age. Shoot, we come into this world constantly drooling and seeking food, why not leave the same way?

As a wise man said recently, "Heck, you probably already are a crummybutgood scout." You probably already have an eye for trying out the downtrodden restaurants that might or might not offer something special, something extra good inside. You probably already have the zeal of the explorer to keep seeking something new, the disdain of the adventurer for those who would prove they are rich and famous by flaunting multiple silver forks, and the fervor of the knight-errant determined to seek out and preserve the holy grill.

So join our round table. Join with us in the Quest by sharing your discovery of worthy new crummybutgood places and helping update our reviews of the old. Share with us your best finds and tell us—briefly—exactly what makes your CBG place so special. Yes, we are looking forward to exploring new towns and cities, but not exactly sure of which ones and how. Please send your reviews and comments to me care of the e-mail address below.

Not that you need an official form to fill out, but here's a reminder of some of the basic information we need.

1. Name, address and phone number for restaurant

_____

_____

_____

2. Proposed C (crummy) and G (good) rating.

_____

3. Why crummy?

_____

_____

_____

4. But what makes it good? (Food, prices, variety of menu, special dish, wait staff, atmosphere, location or something else?)

_____

_____

_____

5. Favorite meal and price?

_____

Send your reviews and comments to Donovan Kelly at crummybut@aol.com, or CrummyButGood, c/o Capital Books, Inc., P.O.Box 605, Herndon, VA 20172.

INDEX OF RESTAURANTS

INDEX OF RESTAURANTS